FEEDING THE MONSTER

FEEDING THE MONSTER

A Story of
Addiction, Destruction, and Recovery

RONALD R. SCHUR JR.

Library of Congress Control Number:		2013914107
ISBN:	Hardcover	978-1-4836-7546-6
	Softcover	978-1-4836-7545-9
	Ebook	978-1-4836-7547-3

This book was printed in the United States of America.

Rev. date: 010/10/2013

To order additional copies of this book, contact:
Xlibris LLC
1-888-795-4274
www.Xlibris.com
Orders@Xlibris.com
136378

To my family, to those brothers and sisters who have suffered like I have suffered, and to those who have suffered at the hands of an alcoholic or addict. I pray for those still suffering and hope that this book may provide some comfort and somehow help in their quest to lead productive, sober lives.

Serenity, courage, and wisdom for all.

**I am at war with myself,
and both sides are
taking heavy casualties.**

—Ronald Schur

INTRODUCTION

As I watched the darkness descend, the distinction between sky and land disappeared. The murky gray color covered the landscape as if a blanket were smothering my existence. It suddenly grew very cold, and although seemingly impossible, I felt more alone than my life ever allowed before. The darkness entered the room, and the depths of my emptiness felt its presence. It brought me back, back so far that I curled up in a corner much like the position I occupied in my mother's womb so many years ago. While familiar questions raced through my frustrated mind that night, I again realized my quest for an answer may never be over. I prayed over and over for God to take me quietly, without pain. I have suffered enough. My prayers went unanswered again.

With the beginning of each day, we ask the same questions. We pray for answers; we beg to be shown the way to a better life. Alone and broken each night, we ask, we pray for a way out—a way to stop the cycle of destruction, loneliness, and shame. Thousands of times I have repeated this conduct, but for so long now, my futile struggle moves me further away from that which I strongly crave to obtain. Each day, my conduct—although aware of it being ill-advised—brings me to a dark and pathetic place. I cannot escape myself. I cannot forgive myself. Hopeless, hollow, and beat-up, I surrender once again in defeat. And so the cycle continues.

My story is not unknown to mankind. It has repeated itself time and time again. So many have experienced it, and although much of it is now understood, it is often still unforgivable upon self-reflection. Only the alcoholic or addict has the ability, due to experience, to completely engage the true depth of its destruction and resulting emptiness although all in its path suffer relentlessly and often without recourse. This book documents, to the best of my ability, my road to addiction, destruction, and recovery.

A man takes a drink,
The drink takes a drink,
And then the drink takes the man.

—Alcoholics Anonymous saying

CHAPTER ONE

My childhood was eventful but probably typical, considering it was the 1960s and early '70s. I had no idea at the time that my father was an alcoholic, and he had no idea that he had a problem or the collateral damage that our family suffered as a result of his diseases. Multiple layers of unawareness do not equal a positive. The spouses, family, friends, and coworkers of alcoholics can all attest to that. So often, the desire of loved ones to help significantly reduces their quality and the sanctity of their life. Sitting by acting unconcerned carries a different, but similar, destructive burden.

My first memory in life was cuddling with my brother under a coffee table while my father, in a drunken rage, screamed and tossed my mother around like a rag doll in our living room. I have relived it in my head so many times. I was probably only three, my brother two. We were unintentional bystanders to the vivid and dreadful accosting of our mother. The violent outburst and physical violence continued on and off during my childhood, without provocation and without warning. I do not remember the content of any one argument (and there were many). Nor do I recall that any argument had any particular purpose—just the rantings of a man at war with himself and those trying to help him, although all fearing each episode and the aftermath. This created a constant state of panic and anxiety for our household for many years.

Does fear really mature into respect? This is a question I have asked myself so many times. My brother and I were terrified of our father. Possibly, fear more often merely creates resentment. My father was physical with us on occasion, with or without provocation, but verbally abusive regularly. His insults still roam around my head at times. I have vague memories of random assaults as a child and more vivid memories of these in my teens. Shortly after my sixteenth birthday, I received a bloody nose because the turkey was overdone and my father dropped it. A common reaction to many of life's twists and turns by my father. I was a punching bag at times whose momentary purpose was to allow my father an outlet. I am still paying the price for his indiscretions.

When I was seventeen, my father threw me up against the car and pummeled me because my tires spun on glare ice in the driveway. That evening, I actually told him that I would kill him if he ever touched my mother, my brother, or me again. I had no idea where I grew the balls to say that, but my father never came at me physically again. I assume I had built up rage from witnessing and being the unfortunate participant of so many insults and assaults. However, our relationship would not heal for many, many years after that. I have many more of these memories from my childhood, but this is not a self-pity party about my childhood; and for every bad memory, I have many fond memories of my childhood. I had mastered the survival technique many kids do to survive such chaotic lives, but a crop of devastation had been firmly planted.

My father was a very harsh man who was short on lectures but quick with deep-cutting, gene-altering insults and random punches—random because there was no predictability to physical assaults or degrading and disparaging comments. So many times, I probably deserved a good smack, but my father did not seem to oblige when appropriate. He was better with my actual indiscretions than he was with the normal triage of parenting. He was full of good intentions but did not have the tools to adequately convey what was actually in his heart. Looking back, I actually feel sorry for him now that I have some understanding of the nature of the disease and the inner destructiveness and chaos of it and a better understanding of how he was treated as a child and through his teenage years. Now that I have crawled on broken glass through hell myself, I realize he was doing the best he could. I now have not only forgiven him, but actually admire the remarkable steps he took to provide a better life for his children and family. Most of his good intentions and positive actions were lost or dwarfed by his violent outbursts. As children, teenagers, and young adults, we have no idea how to deal with such complexities. I am now all too familiar with his struggles including dismal, dreary, and dark actions and thoughts that possess many alcoholics' lives and minds. I now also know the unfortunate cost of the turmoil, destruction, and shame an alcoholic feels. It is often impossible to love and care for others appropriately when you despise yourself and your own conduct. Anger and resentment for yourself make it easy to degrade and hurt others.

Be that as it may (and without the knowledge I now have), I spent most of my childhood and the years going into my adulthood despising him. Ironic—the disease that created and guided my hatred for my father for so many years was quietly growing inside of me and mounting its calculated and cruel attack on me at a very early age, all while I vowed to never be anything like my father. Do I now have sympathy for him solely because I suffer the same disease? Or did I truly forgive him before I knew we shared the nightmare of addiction? I hope the latter. I want the love and respect I now have for my father to have creditability, not be born out of sympathy. I live with that regret and strive not to repeat it. I pray for the same forgiveness from my children.

During my childhood, my father worked at General Electric. This was a time you could expect hard-drinking and cheating spouses, which were apparently socially tolerated. It may have been tolerated because a typical family included a working father and a stay-at-home mother who was almost forced to tolerate all types of abuse because she was financially stuck in a household with her children, sacrificing quality of life for the financial security of her children. Amazing how we, as children, have no idea about the sacrifices our parents make for us. They suffer and cry silently, smile at us, and give us the last piece of pie no matter how hungry they are. It's amazing that so many of my mother's generation put up with so much, gave tremendously of themselves, and took so little so that their children could have opportunities never provided to them. My mother is a prime example of that. My mother's generation had limited employment beyond minimum-wage labor jobs. I believe her generation knew something had to change and worked hard to begin the process of working toward independence and equality to avoid being confined to such a dismal situation.

My father was a cross between the television character Ralph Kramden and Archie Bunker, with a tendency to become violent. However, there was nothing redeeming or comical about his tirades, tantrums, and violent outbursts. That's what society had to offer? This was acceptable? I think I resented the fact that he could be so appropriate and admired in public but, at home, lashed out without notice like a monster smashing the dreams and devastating the delicate egos and personalities of everyone else in the household. I thought I could survive the attacks and insults, but the ones on my mother and brother seem to cut deeper. In retrospect, I obviously was not as strong as I anticipated. My wounds still bleed in many ways.

My memories of my father during my childhood are convoluted and typically bring back anger for the way he parented and, definitely, for the way he treated me, my brother, and our mother. Even at an early age, the condescending nature and screaming, often directed toward our mother, twisted my insides, creating great conflict. When we are born, we naturally love and admire our parents. This created intense conflict in me. How could he treat my mother so horribly? How could he say those things so angrily to such a loving and caring person? We emulate to duplicate our parents' qualities as children. Early on, I gave up on that biologically given commodity. The sad part is that most of this could've been prevented. Our society just was not aware of the depth of destruction of the disease of alcoholism and addiction, and there were not many places someone could go to get help. It was treated more as a personality defect than a disease. I am confident that any admission or help-seeking back then would have been viewed as weakness. Mockery and alienation awaited the alcoholic (desperate or enlightened) then.

Today, movie stars and the rich and famous have paved the way for acceptance and a few days at a facility to address addiction issues. While I spent most of my childhood and teenage years resenting and often hating my father at times, I had no idea that he had demons far worse than I could've ever imagined coursing through his veins, his heart, and his soul. I never considered he had a nightmare childhood with haunting memories and was emotionally and physically scarred from it. He was a product of his environment and of his own hell, was consumed by it, and unfortunately allowed himself to not only be defined by it but duplicated and repeated it.

As children, we were unaware of even these possibilities as an excuse of misconduct. As children, it would not have mattered; forgiveness was not possible at such a young age even had I known. How pathetic that the disease my father had would encourage me to duplicate his most pathetic and damaging qualities later in life. I only knew that his own anger regularly exploded to the detriment of all those in our household. I had no room in my head or heart for excuses.

Just prior to my father's death and afterward, I discovered that my grandfather came home from World War II a decorated war hero who was wounded deeply in many different layers. He received, as I was later told, medals for heroic actions on the battlefield. He came home not only physically wounded but, worse, suffering the ailments that many individuals suffer when they see the atrocities that war has to offer. There was very little discussion in our family households during my childhood about this issue, and it was only upon my grandfather's passing and my father's illness that I started to hear the stories of how tragic the injuries to my grandfather were. Like father, like son? The sins committed by and on my grandfather caused great hardship. My father silently suffered too.

Apparently, for years after he came home, my grandfather would wake up screaming and shaking with sweat and chase my grandmother around in the night, not knowing who she was. My grandfather suffered from horrible dreams and night terrors that must have brought him back to the hell he endured with his comrades on the battlefield while overseas. I was told that the man he was never came home, and a wounded, angry man full of raging and dangerous emotions returned in his place. I am sure that while he fought for our country and watched his friends die, while he killed for his country and almost was killed himself, he had no idea that the baggage he would bring home would forever mold his life and many of his relationships and the relationships of others for generations to come.

It has been reported to me that my father, being the oldest of four kids, seemed to get the brunt of my grandfather's inability to cope with life. I found out in my thirties that my father was regularly beaten, was chained to a garage like a dog, and often was treated nearly as poorly as an animal at a slaughterhouse. My father worked as a child and teenager, and all the money he earned was taken and went to help the family, in between the beatings he received from my grandfather. This, in and of itself, is its own tragic story. However, I only know a small portion of the brutality my father sustained. My aunt confirmed the veracity of this information prior to and subsequent to my father's death. It makes me wonder if it was and is more common than anyone will easily admit. So many heroes with nowhere to go and no place to receive help quietly suffer in their homes while slowly destroying the delicate lives of their children and loved ones, all while not so quietly suffering and struggling with their own demons—demons created as a result of their honorable service.

My father stopped drinking when I was between ages twelve and thirteen. He became my scoutmaster, and I believe it was his attempt to make good for the damage he had caused our family. Even with these good intentions, my father became what I now know as a "dry drunk," and I think his anger grew worse at times. Many times, as a child or young man, I thought that forgiveness was easier when he was drinking or hungover. I could easily point to alcohol and assign it a percentage of the blame. When my dad was violent or otherwise inappropriate. I could not point to the bottle After he stopped drinking, I had lost my scapegoat, and so did he. I held my father accountable, but I had no ability to understand. I simply reacted and judged. He was so cruel at times and so remorseful at others. Cruelty and remorse seem to feed on each other: the yin and yang of hell.

I now completely understand his struggle. I wish I could talk to him again, hold him; maybe we would cry together and share stories about being so emotionally schizophrenic. My father's dying wish was that I put down the bottle, and he pleaded with me as he told me how booze had created so many problems in his life. He must have forgotten I was well aware. During his lectures while he was dying, I never reminded him how my mother, brother, and I spent our lives walking on eggshells, waiting for the next display of insults or violence. That would have been cruel. How strange. I waited years to inflict pain on him, to undermine him, to hurt him. I prayed for the opportunity so many times as a young man, but instead, I became understanding and caring. When my opportunity finally arrived, he was frail and weakened. I gave up on keeping score and simply wanted to help him find some peace, tranquility, and quantification for his life.

When he became terminally ill, he told me a number of times how he wished he could undo the harm that he caused my mother, their marriage, and to our family and that he was truly remorseful. Unfortunately, during this period of time, I was in the grips of the disease but had absolutely no idea that I was an alcoholic. It would be years after my father's death before I would begin to understand. I could not understand the disease until, after years of suffering its symptoms and consequences myself, I surrendered to it and accepted that all the willpower in the world is no match for the strength of the disease, or the monster within that uses anything it can to ensure its feeding.

Prior to my father's death, he seemed to change everything about himself. The years before he passed at the age of fifty-nine, he must have danced with his demons and tucked them away because he became a class act as a father and grandfather. There was much more to it than my forgiveness. He changed; he cared. He held his temper; he complimented and did not angrily criticize. It must have always been buried inside but hidden behind his struggles. I now deeply regret avoiding him and resenting him for so long. He must have been so lonely and ashamed of the way he acted—a kind heart with the inability to adequately show love, almost always stifled by a cunning and baffling disease that destroys in such a cold and heartless manner.

I have now experienced the pain of this conflict. Is it my punishment for being so dismissive of his struggle? Or simply the cruel twist of fate that I inherited the gene that most likely caused the turmoil in his life that made me think so unkindly of him? What a horrible price to pay to finally understand and forgive.

All in all, I actually have many fond memories of my childhood: black-and-white Victrola with Elvis records playing regularly, with a little Dolly Parton thrown in on occasion; Saturday-night *Red Skelton* viewings on a black-and-white television with popcorn or ice cream; cutting and splitting wood for heat; having our own garden for our vegetables; picking berries for homemade jam; homemade french fries; and living in the country where we fished and hiked and enjoyed the wonderful foothills of the Adirondacks in upstate New York. Both my parents supported education, the scouting program, and sports, and my brother and I were actively involved in all of that.

For every bad memory or event, I have many good memories about my childhood. My mother was always loving and caring and made up for the serious shortcomings of my father. They say what doesn't kill you makes you stronger; for many years, I felt strongest when using—obviously misdirection. Was it a coping mechanism? Were the turmoil, beatings, and anxiety from my childhood excuses to drink? There is no doubt many children had far worse childhoods than I did and many did not run to the bottle or worse.

Common backstory, so many options, unless you are an alcoholic-to-be. The beginnings of a disease that used life's turmoil to feed itself? Ironically, it does not matter. My time and energy are—and were—much better spent on getting sober.

Addiction: suicide on the installment plan.

—Alcoholics Anonymous saying

CHAPTER TWO

I was a typical awkward teenager. It was the midseventies, and I wore a silk shirt, had a gold chain, and my parents made me wear plaid pants as they felt jeans were disrespectful. I was a cross between a disco dancer and a Shriner's clown. No wonder why no one got laid in seventh and eight grade in my school. At the time, all I wanted to do was fit in like most young teenagers. I have no memory of who my role models were, but I would like to thank them because I remained a virgin much longer and, as a consequence, avoided the common complication of heartbreak for a few years longer. I was struggling with my identity: who I was, what I was, what I would become, and obviously what path I wanted or needed to take to get there. Being a teenager is not for the faint of heart—a great opportunity for a disease to plant the seed of future devastation. Alcohol, drugs, and addiction feed on these emotions and profit from them. Childhood turmoil and teenage anxiety are very fertile soil for them seeds of addiction.

I wore my hair long, as the residual effects of the hippies from the '70s had some impact on hairstyle. Every part of me was a duplication of others, and I was not alone. In retrospect, when we question who and what we are, we often just simply grab the desirable personality traits and dress habits of those we desire to be like. Maybe this is how we are trained to succumb to marketing through commercials and advertisements. Teenagers are chameleons and are so capable of being molded in every aspect from their surroundings. Vaguely aware of these insecurities, we look to find something in common with all others; we search for something that will ease our discomfort and feelings that we do not fit in and feelings of not knowing who we really are. Sadly, we often look to many others who also share these feelings and confusing emotions. They are often as ill-equipped as we are. It is like trying to hit a moving target that in reality does not even exist, only an illusion. With these wavering principles and insecurities, we search for something to make us comfortable in our own skin, something that is capable of making us that which we see ourselves being and maybe even invincible in some respects. As teenagers, hormones and emotions race and change the rules every day. I wonder if other mammals strive so hard to belong. As teenagers, we want to fit in; as adults, we want to stand out. Is this the path to maturity or just simple individual evolution? We need to evolve into a less painful path for our children's children. Regardless, there is a lot of insecurity on this road.

Like so many before and after me and many to come, at an early age, I found my magic potion—the anti-anxiety, over-the-counter liquid for teenagers. One swig, and my insecurities and apprehension started to disappear. Two swigs and I was the life of the crowd regardless of what I was wearing or the way I felt for days before that moment, telling funny stories and jokes and making people laugh. Three swigs and I had an ego to go along with my newfound comfort level—invincible and popular, at least in my heart and mind. Even when faced with discourse or conflict, I would easily overcome it and brush it off without much reflection when drinking. This was everything I thought I wanted to be, everything I wanted to feel, and like Alice in Wonderland, all I needed was a drink from a bottle to be bigger, smaller, taller, faster, or stronger. Courage, popularity, and comfort level in a bottle. *Wow*! It marketed itself from the first drop, but like everything else, that's too good to be true; it was too good to be true. If I had ever been warned of the dangers, I was dismissive, as the way I felt while drinking triumphed intelligence or intellect.

I spent a good part of the mid—and late seventies buying beer, usually Miller Ponies from a local general store. Miller Ponies had eight ounces of courage and ego in each glass bottle. There were eight in each pack, and they went down quickly, and often in one gulp. Drinking age was eighteen, but if you knew anybody, you could buy beer or get someone to buy it for you. It was readily available, and the drinking age was a very small obstacle to obtaining alcohol. As a result, it was available at almost every teenager function, party, and household. Beer and booze became the social lubricant that allowed an average awkward teenager to fit in and, many of us would argue, to excel socially. I was sold. I was hooked on the result and soon would be hooked on the feeling and, unfortunately, eventually the substance itself.

As a teenager with alcohol coursing through my veins, I became the cocky, arrogant yet self-thought, desirable young man who could date, play sports, get good grades, and be secure enough to stand my ground under any circumstances. It soon became far more than a social lubricant. I could not believe how well my new magic potion seemed to work to silence my fears, cage the squirrels in my head, and remove the turmoil that my earlier teenage years so readily provided. I did not understand how it worked. I was so comfortable with the results that I did not question it nor were there any concerns with any of the effects of long-term use. As human beings, we suffer from this common affliction, often accepting short-term benefit without honestly looking at the long-term consequences. We have done it to our bodies; we have done it to our surroundings and our relationships. Our government officials have done it for years, and we have done it to mother earth, the womb of all mankind. Ironic, I was so angry at my father, had no idea the background to his dysfunction but took my potion gladly when available. I drank from the same fountain of evil but was unaware of the obvious conflict. Hypocrisy is a common trait for people with addictions or on their way to addiction. I loved booze; it loved me, and I spent little or no time in thought about any negative possibilities.

Like most things in life we enjoy, I became complacent with beer quickly, and it was replaced by hard liquor when we had a chance to score some. I had upgraded—a play on words for progressing. I had no idea that I had actually set a train in motion that didn't have any brakes and was traveling in one direction down a steep hill on a course guaranteeing destruction. The seeds of addiction were planted, and I was in its grip thirty years before I even considered that I was an alcoholic or addict. They say that alcoholism is a progressive disease, and I'm proof of that. How could I not have any concept for so many years of the course that had been plotted for me? Raw intellect is no match for addiction.

My junior and senior year in high school, many of us partied almost every weekend. We drank too often, drank too much, and it became a common way of life, a way to socialize, and a way to survive, so we thought. The buzz was a must. I could not imagine fun without it. The thought of it, the hunt for it, the use of it, and the recovery from it became very time consuming. I was abusing the hell out of it at an early age. Even with the early warning signs, I saw nothing wrong with being intoxicated and acting stupid. As young adults, we romanticize alcohol consumption and often select to only recall the fun, not the destructive moments or events.

I actually made it through high school without ever trying any street drug or taking any prescription medicine not prescribed to me. Addiction is a progressive destructive path, and as a result, that would soon end.

Serenity is not freedom from the storm,
but peace amid the storm.

—common AA saying

CHAPTER THREE

My first semester at college was at a local community college fifteen miles from my house. I was the oldest grandchild on my father's side and the first grandchild to attend college of both my mother's and father's families. I think this may have given me a longer leash than I deserved. Actually, I know it did. My parents were proud; I had aspirations and dreams, but they did not include addiction and its repertoire. The road to hell is often paved with good intentions. I have given much creditability to this cliché. I was now the legal drinking age, and alcohol was sold on campus. A freshman could go into any bar and buy a drink legally although still easily obtained by people under the legal age. Alcohol was so readily accessible and acceptable. I drank while in high school although I always worried about going home, and the wrath of my parents was anticipated. Harsh as their wrath was, the consequences did not preclude the drink. However, I had concerns that if I got in trouble, I could not play school sports, and I loved them. Society had little, if any, pressure to act any differently—in the '70s or '80s at least. That was my perception of it. At least where I grew up, that concern forced some restrictions on my alcohol consumption while in high school and while going home to my parents almost every night while in high school. While I was at college and stayed with friends in a place dubbed the Animal House (named after the movie and worthy of the title given to it by many of the partygoers that frequented the house), any self-imposed restrictions I had brought to college with me were quickly and easily removed. I was free to destroy brain cells and my liver without obvious recourse as I had no one to answer to and had quickly surrounded myself with people that drank to excess, just like me. The situation was a dream for an alcoholic-in-training.

Money became the most common restriction regarding my alcohol consumption during this period. However, I had a 1971 Dodge Challenger—fast and loud 318 engine, and it was an obnoxious bright orange color. I met the guys from the animal house who had a little more money than I had, but they had no car. They drank like I did, were vulgar like me, and they laughed like I did. As a result, the restriction on alcohol consumption placed upon me by lack of funds was quickly resolved. I drove; they paid, and we all drank. Problem resolved—another creative way to bring on the drunk. As alcoholics, we are some of the most manipulative and resourceful people you could ever meet.

College in the early '80s was as much about the party as it was about the grades, at least in my self-created mini subculture. The first two years I really had no actual concept what was at stake for my future. I was skating in the grades arena, so my binging and excessive alcohol intake went largely unnoticed, or so I thought. My own brother did mention to my parents that I had crossed the line with my alcohol consumption and conduct. However, the worrying was quickly laughed over when I got my grades, and it was chalked up to "young man's new freedom" theory. Watching sports and playing sports was also important. Both involved alcohol to excess; in fact, almost everything did back then.

I drank hard; I drank often, and I drank to excess regularly my first year in college. With my newfound friends and with the legal age limit now obtained, I was soon to find the bar scene. The next arena for my soon-to-blossom addiction had presented itself with neon lights, foosball tables, pool tables, dart boards, women, and all the booze and beer you could drink. Soon I was staying out with the guys in bars regularly and ended up carrying equipment for a local band and staying to help to break down until 4:00 am regularly—a resourceful way to be required to stay until closing time. Before long, I was working the door at a local bar, often drinking for free while mingling in the bar. I bartended and watched the door as a bouncer—anything to be at the bar where the action and mischief was. Now I was paid to hang out and drink in my newfound favorite place-to-be.

I was playing flag football at college at the time, and in my second year, I met some guys who indicated I should try out for a local semi-pro football team. Soon I was practicing after classes, bouncing and or bartending nights; summers I worked landscaping and installing pools, all while maintaining good grades. I remember thinking during this period, through many hangovers, that as long as I had good grades, the hard-partying life I was living was not a problem. I had no idea I was planting seeds of destruction. Because of work, partying, and school, I would often go on two or three hours of sleep.

Enter drugs.

At first, it was caffeine pills and, soon, speed. *Wow, what a ride*, so I thought. Now I could go to school, play semi-pro football, work nights in the bars, party, still attend classes, and get good grades. I found it heaven on earth. I was hooked on the lifestyle as much as I was becoming hooked on the multiple substances I was putting in my body. I've heard many people say that one intoxicant doesn't lead to another. That is not my experience. No race car driver ever said "That was fast enough, let's not try to go faster." I started with alcohol and then pills to help me stay awake and alert. At least, that was my thought. It seems there is a honeymoon period for addiction and for each substance that I was introduced to in college. But with each new level of intoxicant, any reservations quickly dissipated, and any hesitation that it was wrong on any level also disappeared quickly. I still drank as always, as my drug of choice was alcohol, but now I was dabbling with other intoxicants. I had taken it up another notch—a very regrettable large notch. In retrospect, I was progressing along predictably and normally on the road to full-blown addiction and its unfortunate consequences.

While working in bars, it did not take long until I was introduced to coke. A controlled substance was as easy to obtain as alcohol for minors.

Enter insanity.

So much for the word "controlled." There is nothing that resembles control when doing lines. If it wasn't so expensive, anyone who ever touches it would do it regularly and find themselves in an early grave. I remember reading that animals that were introduced to opiates would go without food or water and would take the opiates to their detriment and early death. At this point in my life, alcohol and drugs were now part of my regular weekly routine. They were readily available at college and openly available in the bars. The availability almost made you forget they were illegal. It was socially acceptable; my friends accepted it. I accepted it. Hell, I even viewed it as mandatory at the time—pre-addiction and addictive logic.

The college bar scene did nothing to persuade me that there was anything wrong with what I was doing. We tend to gravitate to those that act like us or do as we do. It is now obvious that I was lying to myself as I thought my conduct and alcohol and drug habits were acceptable. What a farce. It's like surrounding yourself with five-hundred-pound people and believing that you're thin at 350 pounds. That is what people with abuse or addiction issues do. We surround ourselves with people that act like we do, drink like we do, or drug like we do so that in the few moments of self-reflection that we have a month, we can lie to ourselves and tell ourselves that we're not that bad and that it's all okay. It is like Ted Bundy saying "I'm not so bad if you look at John Wayne Gacy. He killed thirty-eight people."

The disease controls so many aspects of our life, and it is not even possible for us to count the ways in which it affects every single decision we make for so many years. I was an Eagle Scout and an honor student playing semi-pro football, working in the bars, and partying in epic proportions. How naïve is it that I saw nothing wrong with any of it? Addiction feeds easily on our naiveté later on its destructive path, and it also feeds endlessly on denial.

After two years, I obtained my associate degree and went to state school to continue my education and partying. I knew the bar scene well and got a job working weekends and some weeknights at bars at college or back home on weekends. Between the bars, college, my friends, and football, I had plenty of opportunities to drink with others who drank like I did. Beer, shots, pills, lines—whatever it takes to get there. That was the mood. That was the attitude. That was acceptable. There were no rules, just the craving to be drunk or high. My third or fourth year of college simply duplicated my first two. I kept my grades up and based upon that sole fact alone, as I recall, that I'd never seriously considered that I was abusing alcohol or drugs or that I had any issues with alcohol or drugs. The thought of being an alcoholic was not even a remote possibility. I honestly thought that all alcoholics were homeless, sitting on a corner with a cup, begging for money to buy their next drink. Denial is a large part of the disease, and I think not being aware is an early stage of denial. I am convinced that long before denial, there is a level of unawareness that denies logic.

While I was in state school for my third year and fourth year of college, one of the local drug dealers I had partied with many nights until sun up was arrested. He ended up doing local time, and some believe he worked with the local police to set up his suppliers. I have no idea if that was true. He was a really nice guy from an affluent local family, and all he was doing was selling to support his habit—a common occurrence in the drug and addiction world. Then things got really scary. The owner of the bar I worked at the most and partied at the most was arrested for conspiracy to distribute cocaine. Shortly after my senior year, our local town was buzzing over the news. Many of my friends that I worked with and played football with were questioned by the police. My boss allegedly paid someone to go to Florida and bring back a large quantity of coke. The coke never made it home, and the driver of the car sang like a bird when he was told he was facing 8 1/3 to twenty-five for possession and conspiracy. He sang and walked; my boss ended up doing a five to fifteen bid in state prison. That scared a lot of people for a while. Addiction not only denies logic and is a type of insanity, but even with so much at stake, we often romanticize the substance and shun the possible consequences of getting caught. I believe all it did was make the others involved in drug use and the other street pharmacist smarter. Misery loves company, but often, someone's misery is someone else's lesson.

I received my four-year degree with an academic honorary society plaque and bragging rights and entered law school. That is where the hard work, relentless hours of studying, lack of money, my first daughter, and resulting marriage seriously limited my drinking. I still hit it hard on weekends when I could. It wasn't often because I had to work full time my second and third year of law school in a law firm as a law clerk just to get by. My parents worked very hard and were supportive financially to the best of their ability and otherwise; but with their help, some financial aid, scholarships, and loans, I still was required work. I was so focused; I worked so hard and was so productive that I eventually graduated with my juris doctorate. I now had a law degree—another excuse I used to justify that I did not have a problem. There were sporadic episodes of excessive drinking during law school but a small percentage of what it was the first four years of college.

I had a job waiting for me in the firm that I was law clerking for. I had a daughter, a wife, and a law degree, and I was released into the real world, completely naïve about the concept of life on life's terms. I guess I expected life to be easy and the world to sit at my feet and be in awe. I had climbed to the top of a high mountain, and I wanted respect. I deserved it. Hell, I demanded it. How narcissistic. Young and unappreciative of my role in deserving the respect of others and myself, which of course is not what happens. No one told me, nor would I have listened, that life can be hard. Wear a helmet and bull yourself forward. In fact, I was living a reasonably good life, but apparently, I did not know it or appreciate it. My first forty years, I viewed compliancy as a weakness.

I was not in college and the bar scene, so drugs quickly became a thing of the past. However, alcohol, as always my first intoxicant of choice, was readily available and willing to attempt to provide the answers for any of life's quandaries on a moment's notice. It was as much a social lubricant now as it was when I was a teenager and in college. I hung out and made friends with people who would not consider judging me because they acted like me and drank like me. This was not intentional but cannot be reasonably argued as coincidental. This is not to say they were not good people. Many were dear friends who loved, laughed, and cared as I did; others were simply drinking buddies. When you're buying drinks, everyone is your friend. When you're drunk, you think everyone admires you. Just a simple thought process to allow an alcoholic-in-training to continue antifamily destructive behavior.

One is too many,
Twenty is not enough.

—common AA saying

CHAPTER FOUR

Within a year after passing the bar, I purchased a small law firm ten miles from my hometown. My disease was progressing as it does for most others, but I was judged differently and not held accountable because I was viewed as successful to many. I also landed a job with the public defender's office for a regular paycheck and benefits. I knew that if I did not jump on this opportunity to own my own business early in my career that life would soon get in the way and I would never have the nerve to do it. A goldfish grows to the size of its fishbowl quickly and becomes complacent easily. Humans duplicate this conduct. I was soon to have my second child and wanted to provide my children a lifestyle I never had or that I thought I never had. I must have thought that I would replace what I thought I missed out on with money and material things. The American dream. It was sold to me in every magazine I read and every TV commercial I saw. It is practically part of our genetic code. We were sold the story: Your grandparents and their family came here, didn't speak the language, and worked hard so you could live the American dream. Be a good little worker bee, make money, pay taxes, live in peace, and prosper. That is how the story is told and sold, but that is not how it always goes. The opportunity is there if you can avoid the obstacles.

I was very busy and worked many hours, often a hundred hours a week, getting to the office between 4:00 and 5:00 am seven days a week. My mindset was that not only could I not fail but I had to excel and exceed all expectations including my own. I immediately became very competitive—competitive with others and competitive with myself most of all. I have met many successful attorneys, and there is a fine line between their desire to protect their client's rights and the need to simply win for their own sake. Either way, the client benefits. I was now an attorney, practicing law in my own business, and there was little or no room for bars, drugs, or drinking during the week. On weekends when I was lucky, there were family get-togethers, birthday parties, barbecues, and social gatherings that would allow me the opportunity to feed the monster that was growing and gathering strength within me. I think the monster got stronger even when I was not drinking. Not drinking does not mean sober. I believe I filled the loss of my regular drinking with working—one addiction for another. I was so busy that I didn't even really seem to miss the large amounts of alcohol that I had been consuming for so many years. Don't get me wrong, when I had my chance on the weekend, I could pound a case of beer or a bottle of vodka without much effort. I was very proud of myself for how hard I was working but now realize I had simply traded addictions, which I also now know to be a common occurrence with alcoholics and addicts. My newfound addiction was work, and it was consuming me and affecting my life in a similar or parallel way to that which alcohol had previously done. I just had less guilt at first. At least with work, my family received the benefit of hefty paychecks and a comfortable lifestyle.

I was soon appointed the public defender and was heading up the public defender's office. I wasn't thirty years old yet. I was regularly trying cases and working on hundreds of files a year just at the public defender's office. I was fortunate to have tremendously talented and hard-working assistants and enjoyed working with them and wrapped myself in the United States flag and knew I was doing the right thing for many people who were far less fortunate than me. Besides, who was I to judge; most of the people I represented had been caught doing the things I regularly had done for so many years. I was blatantly honest with many of my clients and told them that I walked where they had walked and that the difference was that I had never been caught. I believe that this level of honesty from their lawyer in a suit and tie in a nice office with a law degree hanging on the wall actually almost marketed me although it was unintentional. I had shared many of these personal experiences with my clients so they would know that I was on their team. I was actually pulling for them and was familiar with many of the struggles that led to their requirement for my legal services.

I took each case personal and was obsessed with doing the right thing by my clients and for me. I was still playing semi-pro football, and there were many similarities between the courtroom and the football field. On the football field, I would try to destroy an opponent even when the scoreboard was not in our favor. In the courtroom, this was done with a smile and by outworking your opponent. I learned early on that to achieve the level of success that I wanted as an attorney, there needed to be sacrifice. In a courtroom, making an adversary work hard for a victory was part of their punishment. Of course, I used my long hours and hard work to justify and hit the bottle hard on weekends when I had an opportunity. I was working many hours and worked hard. I started to give myself a longer leash for my alcohol consumption on weekends. I wonder if "I was immersed in work" was another excuse to earn some leeway on the weekends to enable me to have alcohol coursing through my bloodstream. I was slowly getting back to my alcohol-use quantity from my college days on weekends.

My private practice took off—in part due to very hard work and some luck, in part due to my success in the public defender's office, in part due to social functions, and in part because my newfound weekend drinking buddies and social functions were business owners and employees in a position to spread my name in a small community to their colleagues and friends. This was absolutely unintentional, and I'm sure I provided them the same service. Before long, I was hanging with other successful business owners and businessmen and women on weekends who drank like I drank. The drugs were not far behind. A suit and tie, a wine glass, and a martini or scotch glass do not exclude narcotics. I often thought that a higher class of drunks excluded drugs, but I was dead wrong.

I would learn a lesson about many drinking buddies later in life. They are good-time Charlies, and many of them are only faithful to you and a true friend while the booze and stale jokes are flowing. Hypocrites drinking the potion to help them avoid any true self-reflection. Why not, I was bathing in hypocrisy myself. Besides, when a buddy gets sober, it threatens their way of life. A sober and clean member of the pack might grow a conscience and tell all that sobriety is good and might even share the deep and often dark secrets of the drunken pack. There are many casualties of surface friendships when someone tries to get sober or accomplishes sobriety. They were afraid their wives would learn of all the misconduct—the drinking, drugging, and cheating. Drinking, drugging, and cheating go hand in hand. They feed off each other. They all fed the monster.

While in high school, then a two-year college, continuing at a four-year college and law school, and now in the professional world, I seem to always find people who acted like I acted and drank like I did. I had no idea until years later that the alcohol was choosing many of my friends. There is a process of elimination of possible friends when you abuse alcohol and/or drugs. What a shame, how many worthy relationships did I pass up because they did not abuse intoxicants? I do not remember hanging out with anyone other than those who drank like me. Many people can drink recreationally and never let the monster lose. That, unfortunately, was not my experience. With every drink that I ever had, my Mr. Hyde came a little closer to the surface.

In our small town, I started to have a reputation of the hard-working young lawyer with the young family who partied hard on weekends. My friends and I were wild, loud, obnoxious, and often inappropriate, but we were all given a lot of latitude as we all worked and were successful in our respective businesses or business ventures. It took a few years to establish these friendships and social pattern, and they continued with frequency and intensity for about ten years. We were masterful at coming up with reasons to get together for social gatherings on weekends, bringing spouses and friends and family and children together while we drank hard and laughed. We worked hard, and on weekends, we would get our families together in part as an excuse to drink and in part out of the guilt that we would feel if we drank without them in the other room or without the kids playing in the yard or other room. Bar drinking was few and far in between and deemed to be inappropriate, so we confined most of our drinking to the social gatherings at each other's homes. That, of course, changed over time.

The harder I worked, the more money I made. The closer I got to my drinking buddies, it seemed the further I drifted from my wife at that time. We were actually not ever very close, but both of us loved our children, and we parented in a parallel manner. She had her responsibilities and she provided care for our children, and I had what seemed to be separate responsibilities with regard to our children, as well as other obligations. It was like offense and defense in football—same team but on the field at different times. Together, we were a reasonable team raising the children, but beyond that, we really didn't spend any time together alone. Nor did it appear that I desired that. I much preferred the guys and family members who drank on weekends so that I could drink to excess. My wife was in the other room with her friends or family members, and the kids were playing, so I truly believed at the time I was fulfilling my responsibility to my family. I was technically with my family.

No remorse until years later. I was not at work and I was physically with them, although my focus was on alcohol consumption and intoxication. I may have been present, but I was absent in many respects and failed to understand this until many years later. It started to sink into my thick head on my second child's fifth birthday. My wife at the time put out a photo album of his first five years. I do not think there were two photos where I was in. I mentioned it, and an honest answer presented itself.

"You are always working."

I had missed many of the magical moments of his life and his brother's and sister's lives, but I really did not like being home with my wife. And besides, working was easier. I was a workaholic, and work was also a great way to avoid life. Booze does that too. Work hard, drink hard, and avoid much of the day-to-day turmoil.

This pattern of silence started to lead to marital turmoil, and the way I dealt with it was working more hours, coming home later from the office, and drinking even harder on the weekends. I remember telling my friends that I really needed to get together this weekend as things were not good at home, and I could use a get-together—just another aspect of life that I used to drink and not deal with the challenges of my existence. Of course, the marriage was over long before we declared it over. But before its slow miserable death, I regularly needed to let loose a little bit and not be stifled by the deafening silence of my dying marriage. Ironically, although my marriage was soon to formally be a casualty, many of the seeds were planted long before we realized we had issues, even before alcohol became the primary function on weekends. I used alcohol to tolerate an otherwise intolerable situation in my marriage. Which came first, the intolerable marriage or the alcohol abuse/addiction?

An expectation is often a predetermined resentment.

—common AA quote

CHAPTER FIVE

I now believe my first marriage was doomed from the start. I love my first four children dearly, but I have now discovered and realized that I was never really close with their mother. I did not know that while we lived together. I did not have anything to compare that relationship to and thought our relationship was normal. Silence and painful togetherness is not a good marriage. Maybe that is normal for divorced couples? I do not blame her. The chemistry just wasn't there. There may not have been room for me to be a law student, then a lawyer and business owner, a father and a spouse. That may sound like a sad excuse, but it was my dismal sense of limits of time and love. Probably, my imperfect triage of responsibility added to this abyss. I never really included her in these things and never really thought to try to. Any attempt was met with criticism and conflict, and a lot of it. I wonder if it was because we never really connected or shared the same dreams and goals. Was it more likely that the selfishness of addiction would never allow me to let her in?

I seem to have everything I really wanted—successful business, many wonderful friends and drinking buddies, and now four beautiful children to share my life with when I was not working. I had so much to offer my children by example. Sadly, they pay attention to the admissible and not the admirable conduct—somewhere in between the cost average the good and bad. I never intended to be an average father. But the scales of young lives grow ever forgiving with age. I thought my life was full and complete even though my marriage was more of a convenience at this time. This was the calm before the storm. My intact family was quite a damper on my alcohol consumption.

At this point, I spent the last two decades planting seeds for a full field of alcoholism and addiction and practiced over and over with increasing intensity as the years went by. At around thirty-six years old, my father started to have medical problems, and we soon discovered that he had cancer. I went to many doctor's visits with my father and my mother as I was self-employed and could take time. For a while, we thought it was operable and that he would be fine. As he got sicker, I spent more time with my father and mother and his doctors. My wife pulled away from me, and it was obvious that the relationship was in serious jeopardy. In fact, at a time when I was hurting and felt that I actually needed someone, and months after building an expensive and extravagant house to fix a dying marriage, she told me she wanted a divorce. She waited until I came home from my father's cancer treatments. Timing isn't everything, but this timing was about as bad as it gets. That night I drank until I blacked out. There was a retirement dinner for a local judge, and I tipped over and went to the bottle, and I stayed there for many years. It solved nothing, but I forgot about my problems for a short period of time. At least I thought I forgot; blackouts are a short reprieve for life's hurdles.

There was a short period of time I tried to behave to fix it, but it seems like we could never get on the same page. It was dead; resentment had built, and the end was near. It didn't take long for any hopes of the marriage surviving to be extinguished and heavy resentment to set in. Oddly, even though I did not want to be married to her, the concept of my marriage being over during my father's illness and not having every night with my children destroyed me emotionally. I had held on for years to something that was never there and now used its end as a reason to strive for intense and frequent intoxication. Ridiculous, yes, but a convenient excuse at the time.

We found out that my father was terminally ill, and I started to spend quite a bit of time with him and included him in my weekend excursions when I could. My father was well liked by my drinking buddies, and we even started going to lunch, playing cards, drinking heavy, all while spending time with my father. My father had not drank in years, and I think he was so happy to be spending time with his oldest son and his buddies, knowing that he didn't have much longer to live. He did not say much about our alcohol consumption. He didn't say too much about the drinking at the time but had a lot to say the last month of his life. I am sure he was afraid I would reject him when he needed our relationship more than ever, and he even became a designated driver at times for us. Everyone knew he was sick; everyone knew he was dying, but it wasn't discussed. If anyone had seen us having lunch or dinner or at a social gathering, they never would've guessed that my father was terminally ill. They also never would have guessed the nature of our relationship the first thirty years or so of my life.

A few months before my father's death, my parents' house burned down. I had my parents move into my home for a short period time, but my father was very sick, and between the chemo, the vomiting, the treatments, and the medicine, he wasn't doing very well. All four kids were asking questions, and I had no answers other than grandpa was sick. They were very close to my father, and I believe he did not want them to witness his steady and painful decline of health. My mom and dad found a small place to stay while their home was being rebuilt. My father would never make it back to his house. I was sleeping in a separate bedroom prior to my father and mother moving in. I was back in a separate bedroom immediately after they moved out. I could not tell my father that my marriage was over, that I'd suspected my wife of infidelity, and that I had no idea how I would survive financially. He had enough on his plate, and I could not burden him and my mother with my impending issues. I was drinking regularly and hard and, now and then, in the bars too. I started to like the bars again, and the restraints that kept me out of them were now gone, at least in my mind. My children needed me more than ever, but I was drinking my potion, feeding the monster, and regrettably not home for my kids nearly as often as I should have. These regrets will be with me to my last breath.

Just prior to the fire, my uncle, my mother's brother and one of my father's best friends, was killed in an accident while at work. My aunt called me and told me she was a widow and knew the fragile state of affairs for my family. She asked me to go sit with my parents and tell them my uncle Tom was dead. My parents had planned one last trip to Georgia to see my uncle and aunt. They were leaving in a few days for one last trip together before my father could no longer travel. My dad and my uncle were going to go to a NASCAR race, and my uncle had some excellent tickets. It was all he could talk about for weeks. I was so happy one of his dreams would soon be fulfilled. His bucket list was short but very important to him. My father was an avid NASCAR fan and was so excited. What more could you throw at him? I left my law firm and drove to my parent's home. I sat with them. I died inside a thousand times in those few minutes before I told them. My heart was broken. I questioned God's existence. They each cried hysterically and clung to each other. My father lost the best man at his wedding, his friend; my mother lost her friend and brother. They were struggling with my father's impending death and now this. I remember being completely numb that evening. Nothing more upsetting than thinking God was pissing on your father's grave, months before he would occupy it. I could hardly talk; I was hurting so bad for my mom and dad and could do nothing for them but be there and love them. I was convinced this was not enough. This may have been the moment my father surrendered to his cancer and final fate. I saw it in his eyes. He seemed to lose his fight. The little spark he had left was extinguished.

During this period time, I was reintroduced to the bar scene. I had given up on my marriage, was hurting from the thought of the loss of daily contact with my children, and was hurting at the thought of loss of my father and the events that brought pain and misery to my parents. After all those years of despising him and not liking him, he was now a very good father and friend and grandfather, and I actually enjoyed spending time with him before he got sick and also while he fought his illness with courage and integrity. Why couldn't he have treated me like this the first thirty years of my life? Like the man I got to know the last few years of his life, why not that quality of parenting and friendship for me the first three decades of our relationship? I was full of emotion. I was sensitive and hurting. I was fighting all my demons alone, or so I thought. And at the time, I was also angry that my dad, the one I always wanted, emerged just in time to slowly and painfully die right before my eyes. Would I have cared nearly as much ten years before? I questioned whether he somehow knew that he had cancer or if the cancer itself had actually changed something inside him because it was like a switch was flipped in the last five years of life. He was the father and friend that I had imagined in my head for so long. He became the husband my mother deserved, and in the last two years, she was his nurse, taking care of all the nasty chores that cancer, surgery, and a colostomy bag have as challenges. God blessed my dad with my mother. While I had mass symptoms of my disease that were evolving over the years, now with all this going on, my disease tapped me on the shoulder, whispered in my ear, and made it clear that I needed it, that I needed to feed the monster, and that I needed all the booze or other intoxicants I could drink or use. I was wounded and weak, so I complied.

I was so distraught with the fact that my family would no longer be intact, that I would not be there to tuck my children in every night. There must be a security about knowing that your children are home when you come through the door at the end of a long day, even when you're only spending one or two hours quality time with them. I realize I was already mourning the loss of the family unit. Some would argue I was celebrating it with the amount of booze I drank. But my father had to die first. Callous as that sounds, enough was being dealt with by my parents. Only after my father's death could I disclose the next painful chapter for our family. The circumstances created a feeding frenzy for the monster gaining strength inside of me because I had not surrendered to the power of the monster, because I had no idea I suffered from a terminal illness and addiction; instead, I fed it, fertilized it, made it grow, rather than combat it. The monster fed on my life's circumstances, and I obliged it completely.

When the only tool you have
is a hammer,

Every problem begins to
look like a nail.

—Abraham Maslow

CHAPTER SIX

The last few months of my father's life, I would drink a lot. I would drink with others. I would drink late in my bedroom and, for the first time, sometimes alone. This was the first time in my life I would drink by myself. I always looked at alcohol as a social lubricant; anyone who drank alone was using alcohol adverse to its intended purpose. Of course, any rule I have had regarding alcohol changed as my disease progressed. I was basically living in one room—my bedroom—in the house to avoid my wife, as much as possible avoiding the conflict that was building as was the resentment and apparently our seething hatred for each other. She had no compassion for what I was going through, and so we turned it into an asshole contest. As I previously indicated, I'm very competitive, and I am quite sure to this day that I won the asshole contest. There were some nights I did not even come home. Sometimes, I would come home until breakfast time the next day. My kids would hang out with me until bedtime regularly, and we were actually having fun when I was home. I refuse to talk trash about my soon-to-be ex-spouse, but the kids were very aware what was going on. My conduct and her conduct was the equivalent of trash talk. The kids were hurting too as they knew their parents' marriage was over and that their grandfather was dying. I believe that the concept or actual consequences of both or either were still far from their comprehension. Short term, children seem more resilient with life's ups and downs. Long term, as I have learned, they are injured forever, and the lasting effects and long-term consequences are never truly known. I was squandering my soul to addiction, and I know I had less to offer than I thought.

They called my bedroom the apartment, and we would joke at dinner about it, and the kids would say "Are you going to be home tonight, Dad? We want to come over to your apartment." They regularly spent their evenings with me in my separate bedroom when I was not on a barstool. During this period time, I would drink after the kids went to bed, at times. I wasn't sleeping well, and I was an exhausted shell of a man many days. Drinking often lifted my energy level for short periods of time with the obvious consequences of more exhaustion when I came down. My disease was talking to me. Hell, it was singing to me. It made me promises that I now know it could not keep; it begged to become my best friend and offered to be the most reliable friend I could have, and no matter what time of day or where I was, it promised that it was ready to help me, listen to me, absorb my troubles, and relieve me of pain. My disease became my go-to guy, but the reality was it was actually the proverbial snake in the apple tree of life. I had no idea where I was headed. With the lies and deceit from my disease, I marched into the garden, ate the apple, and then screamed "Give me more!" And the serpent complied with a smile because it was satisfied. It was gaining ground. I was feeding the monster, and it was very hungry. I would do this over and over and over again for years—loving the high and hating the low. Active addiction does not allow you to learn from your mistakes, and you will repeat them over and over. Literally, a form of living hell you cannot escape without complete surrender to the most incomprehensible power of the disease.

I still had some reservations or restrictions on my drinking. I had a little self-respect left and a very small amount of self-control. I demanded of myself that I could not get fall-down-piss-my-pants drunk in front of my children. Wow, what a goal. My parents and loved ones would be so proud. As a result, I would often sleep on a buddy's couch not coming home until morning. I felt that this was much better than coming home between 2:00 and 4:00 am highly intoxicated and risk my kids seeing me. I was now at a point where almost every single time I drank, I was highly intoxicated, and I was starting to have blackouts regularly. This is about the time that any possibility of recreational drinking was gone. I now believe I was officially entering full-blown alcoholism and addiction. It is a progressive disease, and I was progressing. Whenever you're on a barstool intoxicated, many other misbehavers are regular. Drinking and drugging go together. However, I still had no concept that I had a problem, that I was abusing alcohol and drugs. There was no doubt that I was an alcoholic whose life was now completely in the grips of the disease that had taken so many lives and ruined the quality of many others, but I had no idea. How could I exhibit so many symptoms of a disease and not have a clue I was an alcoholic? That, as I now know, is one of the major symptoms—denial. The disease knows it is at risk once someone says "Hello, my name is Ron, and I am an alcoholic." I was drowning my sorrows and combating the sadness and misery in my life. How selfish, my children were hurting too. I was pissing away my legacy with booze and drugs. I was busy looking for answers at the bottom of a vodka bottle when

I should've been looking harder and more often at the 2x3 photo of my kids in my wallet. When I was sober, I was a good father. When I was drinking, I simply avoided being around my children. When I drank at this point in my life, I was on a mission. I wanted to get from zero to highly intoxicated as quickly as possible. I started drinking straight vodka with a few ice cubes. Prior to that, I had made the normal progressions—beer, wine, then booze mixed with club soda or juice, drugs, and then straight booze, sometimes right out of the bottle.

After about a year of heavy drinking and this repeat cycle and although actually growing closer with my children as I spent high quality time with them often without interruption or the demands of a dead marriage, it was time for me to move out. The tension in the home started to seriously affect our ability to enjoy our children when we were together, and that had now bled over to our time without each other and the kids. We did not seem to mind staying in the same household as long as we could quietly suffer and enjoy time with our children separately. But as the conflict grew, as the tension mounted, and as the children became more and more aware of the destiny of our marriage, someone had to fall on the sword and leave. Although I was drinking heavily when I drank, considering myself a happy binge drinker, I worked so many hours I decided that I'm the one who must move out and let the kids stay in their home as long as we could afford it. I am sure to this day I would have made different choices if I had not been drinking so hard. I actually looked forward to the freedom to drink without consequence, or so I thought. There is always a consequence. Drinking like I was, you pay later, like it or not. I never looked at the price tag. I was completely unaware of the price I would pay or the heavy casualties I would suffer. I never considered the consequences to my loved ones, to those beautiful children I had such a high responsibility to. I am now convinced that booze should come with two price tags: first, the short-term costs (amount in dollars) and second, the long-term and likely costs (money, job, home, children, etc.).

Prior to moving out, I extended my possible drinking days from Thursday through Sunday night. I may not have drunk each Thursday through Sunday, but I was hitting it hard two or three of those four days and making myself absent from my emotionally unsatisfying and emotionally painful home. This was the time that she could use to spend with our children. That's what I told myself. I actually convinced myself I was being unselfish and sharing the children when I went out for the evening. It seemed fair on paper: drink three or four days a week and the other three or four days a week spend quality time with my children. Logical?

One day, my brother and I went up to see my father when his time was short. His eyes were different, and he was slurring his speech, and we knew something was seriously wrong. My father, being the trooper that he was, was still making plans to spend more time with my brother and I and my mother. He had continually told us during his illness to take care of ourselves as he had caused his own fate by not going to the doctors. We heard this lecture again that day; it was the last time as I recall. We talked to my mom and called the doctor, and they had us bring him to the hospital. I remember that when my brother and I were leaving and standing in the driveway, it was a sunny and nice day, and one of us looked up and saw a hawk or eagle circling over the place that my father was staying. We both started crying. We knew the end was very near, and the significance of the circling bird was overwhelming to us. Our father was our scoutmaster and was also involved in the Order of the Arrow and taught wood badge. My father was an avid admirer of eagles and hawks. In our Boy Scout experience, we learned that it was not uncommon for a hawk or eagle to circle in such a manner as a basic honorary send-off to someone dying. Indian lore was part of our experience. At least, this is what both of us thought; it was a sign. The circumstances confirmed what we actually knew; we knew it in our hearts for a while, but now our minds followed. Our father would only be with us for a few more hours or days.

We drove him to the hospital for the last time and spent the next nine days at his bedside, with hospice and many family and friends while the disease shut down his kidneys and ravaged his already weakened body. The outpouring of support from the community, our family and friends, and people from the scouting program was welcomed but made the thought of him being gone worse. My father was the first parent of our little social pack to die, and none of us were prepared to deal with it. My mother was beside herself with grief and seeing her so broken up destroyed me. I was hurting, but I was sure that I could get by. I would just busy myself with working and parenting. But upon my father's death, what did my mother have? She would be alone in the house that was being rebuilt due to the fire, with nothing but memories and the thought of what they had planned but would never enjoy. I think it was easier to dislike my father than to see his and my mother's retirement dreams smashed by cancer and his impending death. He had only been retired a few months before he was diagnosed with cancer. I shuddered at the thought and could not contain how deeply I hurt for her, for my father who had changed his ways and had many good and honorable dreams to share with my mother, for my children who came to see him on his deathbed and gave him pictures and hugged and kissed him for the last time. In addition to the most intense emotions I've ever had, none of them positive at the time, my marriage was over, and I would soon be moving out of my home and going through the financial and emotional crisis that divorce has to offer. As an attorney who regularly represents people who go through divorce, I know about the multiple layers of devastation that people suffer in the breakup of their family and the division of their children and their finances. I used these experiences to justify my drinking and drugging. With all my success, I had not learned to accept life's challenges maturely.

I cried more that nine days my father was in the hospital than I think I've cried my entire life. I leaned on my friends, and they were wonderful to me during this period of time. But I still felt sorry for myself. I felt like I had been excommunicated from life. Who had the right to do all this to me? What had I done to deserve this? I have spent my life helping other people in and out of a courtroom. I really couldn't share much with my wife, not necessarily her fault, as our marriage for all practical purposes was over, and I would not lay bare my heart at her feet. Alcoholics can be very stubborn. Active alcoholics are selfish and shortsighted. I could not lean on my mother as she was hurting beyond belief, and she had no idea that my marriage was over and that divorce was the next step for our family. My brother was hurting as badly as I was; my children were distraught at the impending loss of their grandfather, and so I internalized all this and felt dead and all alone. Ironically, I was surrounded by dozens and dozens of people who were caring, loving, and compassionate. My disease, the disease I share with so many, was again tapping on my shoulder, telling me that it would help me get through all this pain and devastation. I should have been thankful that I had four wonderful and healthy children, a thriving business, a wonderful family, and many wonderful friends, but my focus was on my misery. If I was thankful, I could not justify the drinking and drugging. I did not count my blessing; I anchored myself on the misery that allowed me to withdraw and drink and continued the feeding frenzy of the monster.

Sobriety is a unique commodity.
You cannot buy it.
You cannot sell it.
And if you are fortunate enough
to have it, you need to share it
to keep it.

—unknown
(common twelve-step saying)

CHAPTER SEVEN

I've now moved out of the marital residence upon the promise that I would have no problems seeing our children whenever I was not working. We had agreed to share the children equally, or close to equally. This of course only lasted a few weeks. Coincidentally about the same time, another man was swimming in the pool I had built and was there to tuck my children in at night. As much as I was happy that I wasn't in the marital home or in the same house with my wife anymore, the thought of someone else around my children while I worked hard to pay for everything was adverse to anything good in my life. More fuel for my resentments, more resentments to justify the drink. I wonder what I expected. We were at a point where we could not meet and talk civil to each other, so why would I think that I could move out and that we could work together for the benefit of our children? I've seen this scenario so many times with my clients but never thought that it would happen to me. It was obvious to me that although my wife wanted nothing to do with me or could I bear the thought of another day living in the same home with her, her dislike or hatred for me at that time outweighed her love for our children. Almost the minute that I moved out, she was sharing adult issues with our children, much of it blatant misrepresentations, but of course never shared any of her wrongdoings or shortcomings. I wonder how the kids felt. Were they confused with a stranger, days after I moved out, at their home? This is typical in a divorce, but I was confident that we would rise above that and do what was best for our children. My father had died; I moved out of my home. I was no longer tucking my children into their beds at night, and of course, my friend, Mr. Vodka, and all his buddies were waiting for me and prepared to absolve me of my sins and my pain. Stage set, plot obvious, cliché story line.

I was staying at my mother's, including when I had my children. When I was with them, I was solely concentrating on their well-being and shared some of the most wonderful times with them during this period of turmoil in my life. There was some semblance of normalcy as the weight of the dead marriage had been lifted and the curtain of discomfort from my soon-to-be ex-spouse in the other room no longer existed. She probably felt the same? I did not drink when I had my children at this time but hit it hard when I didn't. In my mind, this brought me to the conclusion that I still had some type of control over my alcohol consumption. What a lie. I still had little or no control whenever alcohol touched my lips. At this point, I drank to intoxication every single time I drank. There was no longer any in-between. We both hired lawyers, and the divorce would soon start.

When I received the divorce papers, they accused me of everything but molesting my children. I was accused of being an alcoholic and drug addict, of beating my children, and of other horrendous conduct. Had my soon-to-be ex-spouse completely pardoned herself of our/her wrongdoing? It is almost impossible to disprove a negative and even harder to fight delusions. The part about alcohol and drinking to excess I would at least give some credibility, but I wanted everyone to know that the circumstances of life had set that train in motion. I wanted the world to know of the misfortunes in my life that brought me to the comfort of a bottle. A barstool and a bar were a great podium for my defense. Living the excuse fueled more drinking. Unfortunately, it's required in the state that all divorce papers are filed in the clerk's office. I was confident that everyone in the courthouse, where I worked regularly, had read the papers and the accusations. One of the more valid excuses I had to drink more. I hurt or was seething with anger every minute of every day and felt lost in life except for when I was with my kids or drinking. When I drink, all my concerns, my cares, the trauma I had endured, even the trauma that I caused myself would dissipate into an intoxicating fog and soon disappear into my blackout. How could I have convinced myself I was having fun when I often could not remember the second half of the evening? A lot of people drunk text or drunk dial when intoxicated. I started having long talks with God—I guess I was drunk praying. Thankfully, most of the prayers I had during this period time were not granted. Like Garth Brooks song, thank God for unanswered prayers.

At a time when I thought that I lived a horribly dismal existence, I met the love of my life. She was working in a bar restaurant that I frequented. I'd gone there because the owners were my clients and because they served alcohol and as much as I could drink. I started talking and flirting with her and immediately considered her a likely candidate to spend some time with. I quickly gathered the sense that I actually stood a chance with this young lovely lady. In talking with her and flirting with her, I discovered that she was nineteen years younger than me. This was no barrier, and I was actually intrigued by how young, beautiful, and vibrant she was. I found out from one of her friends that she had a Sunday off and asked her if she'd like to go out to dinner. She accepted, and for the first time in a long time, I felt alive when I wasn't intoxicated. I found some hope that there could be positive things my future. It amazes me that something as simple as a beautiful woman saying yes to a dinner date could create such positive emotions for someone who had been down for so long. My mind raced with excitement, and I could not contain myself at the concept of a date with this young, gorgeous lady. Hell, she was barely older than my oldest daughter. I called a number of my friends and told them what had occurred. I acted like a kid who just found out he had a date to the prom. It had been over fifteen years since I had been on a date. Shit, I wondered if I would make a fool of myself. My excitement outweighed my anxiety, and I could not wait.

On our first date, we went for sushi and drank sake. I immediately felt connected and honored to be out with her. Halfway through dinner, she left her side of the table and sat next to me. We held hands, and the owner of the sushi bar took a photo of us and told us we made a beautiful couple. A couple? I had only been out on a date for a few hours and already had feelings that I thought were long dead. She may never know how much just talking with me, laughing, and touching me meant. After dinner, we went to a bar and had a few martinis. We continued to talk and laugh. All my problems, or so perceived problems, disappeared when I was with her that night. I remember thinking I could get used to this. I drove home, intoxicated from the wonderful experience and the drinks. We immediately started talking and seeing each other every day, and it was honestly love at first sight.

I kept waiting for the puppy love to end and the boredom of a normal relationship to rear its ugly head. Luckily, that did not occur. The newness of our relationship brought us to many bars, many restaurants, weekend excursions, and social gatherings most of which involved alcohol. She worked in a bar restaurant, so I would go to see her and sit at the bar and drink until she got off from work. She really didn't know much about my past but I was the life of the party, quick with a joke, and bought as many drinks as others had bought for me or her. It was an exciting and fun time, but of course, we now know it was simply a perpetuation of my disease.

I waited awhile to introduce my newfound love to my children. I was afraid they would reject her. I was concerned that they were not ready. I did not want to introduce them to someone and have her dart out of my life, leaving me and the children reeling from the experience. My kids had been through enough. When I introduced them to Kristin, we started with the typical daily excursions: pizza, movie, mall, and other fun things. This was what I told my clients to do for years. It worked. We all had fun, and my kids took to her immediately. I honestly think they were happy to see me smiling and laughing. I am sure they had the same feelings about their mother and her new relationships. Even though the divorce papers were ugly, this may have been a sign of things to come. I had hope that things would smoothen out and all of us could be happy and move on with our lives. There had been such a long period of no love, no communication, and nothing but pain and bad memories.

Apparently, after dating a few men, my soon-to-be ex-wife decided I wasn't such a bad guy and started to indicate she wanted to try to reunite the family. I could not even fathom the concept of going back to the way we were living. With everything I've been through, I was actually madly in love with someone who treated me as if I had scripted the relationship with my own pen and paper. For a short period time, my soon-to-be ex-spouse courted the idea of reuniting and sent me flowers, cards, and dropped off coffee to my office. Did she forget what she put in those divorce papers? She accused me of heinous conduct. What was she thinking? I was convinced it was solely about money. She had the kids call me Christmas morning and ask me to move back in. They said, "Mom said it is all right." They were so excited. Of course, when I declined, some problems started. However, the minute that she realized that I would never come back, the insults and the adult conversations with the children continued. With that going on, I had to be very careful about my relationship with my future wife, Kristin. My children told me and Kristin that if it wasn't for her, their parents would be together and I would've been there Christmas morning when they opened up the presents. The weaning-in-process between my children and Kristin had a major setback. I would not be forced to choose between Kristin and my children. There needs to be rules in every war, and my wife at the time had violated every rule. Life's drama often assisted alcohol consumption.

As Kristin was much younger than me, we made the decision that she would not parent the children or be their quote unquote stepparent. She was in a minimal place of authority and was to be their friend. She was only to report serious misconduct to me. I wanted to avoid what I call the stepparent syndrome in many divorces. I call it a syndrome because many parents who meet another love allow the new love to act as a parent to their children who are, of course, defiant as they already have two parents and typically look at the parent's new love as the reason why their parents are no longer together. Understanding children makes this thought process simply common sense. All children want their parents together. It is their number one wish. I believe their second wish is that their parents would be happy together. As many of us know, wish number one is often exclusive of wish number two, and wish number two is often not possible even if wish number one is.

Kristin and I were together for about one year when my oldest daughter moved in. She was sixteen, and I welcomed her company in our house. She and I had some rough years due to the fact that at approximately thirteen, she started speaking a different language, and I could not, for the life of me, communicate rationally with her. However, as soon as she turned sixteen and moved in, it was magical, and we became very close. I believe that I felt vindicated in some respects that one of my children moved in and was living with me and that I was parenting her daily. I pulled back on my alcohol consumption for a period time, but that was short-lived. She became employed as a waitress and worked many evenings. Free time to drink.

About six months later, I was blessed again when my oldest son moved in. I now have two of our four children living with me and felt even further vindicated. I soon would become very comfortable with the older children living with me, see my other children every other weekend and when I could during the week, but I was still binge drinking. My relationship with Kristin was so new. I was trying hard to come home at a reasonable time and often with her. I also had two older children who I was confident would be awake when I came home and had to be standing and able to speak. I struggled hard with these responsibilities and, for a period of time, actually had some control, on occasion, over my drinking. Some control is dangerous because it gives the false impressions you do not have a problem. It allows you to continue to lie to yourself that you are not an alcoholic. Some control is very dangerous and only delays the surrender that saved my life.

Similar with every other level I achieved on my race to full-blown alcoholism, these restraints faded into the obscurity of the disease, and I was soon coming home hours after Kristin would come home after dinner and often in the early morning hours even though my two oldest children lived with me. I promised myself that with my newfound love and my two children living with me that I would start pacing myself, drink responsibly. Willpower and good intentions are worthless when staring into the eyes of alcoholism. Addiction trumps good intentions. I had no idea what I was up against, but I was convinced that the local boy who made good in small law firm who was madly in love and parenting two children every day and four children many days of the week and alternating weekends could put this "habit" in check. I thought I had some control. I must have started to have thoughts that I had issues with alcohol, but my denial was still very strong.

Swans don't swim in sewers

CHAPTER EIGHT

For the first time in a very long time, things seem to be going my way. I was in a new relationship; I was madly in love, and two of my children lived with me. I was seeing my other two children regularly. Now that I look back, this was the first of period time someone regularly called me to task on my drinking. Previously, many people commented on how much I could drink, but I saw that as a trophy—a badge of accomplishment, a challenge for the next time. I now remember regularly telling Kristin that I was just drinking to help me get by during this tough period in my life. Actually, the rough period in my life was over, and all that was left of it was some financial matters with the divorce. Considering what I had been through, this was literally nothing in comparison. My disease had me hang on to that terrible period of turmoil, bringing me to this point. In reality, things were going my way and in a big fashion, but I could not grasp that concept. Being grateful and relieved obviously jeopardized my drinking and would require self-reflection or honesty with myself that I was not prepared to have. There must've been some minor revelation that I had a drinking problem or I never would've indicated to Kristin that I would stop once the divorce was over. I had more than enough reason to put the bottle down and not act like the monster that was growing within me. I had some realization at this point that there was something evil and devastating lurking within me. Satan's tapeworm occupied my soul, and in its feeding frenzy, I was losing all that mattered. Had I understood it to be a disease, maybe I would have asked for an alcohol demon exorcism much sooner. Again, denial feeds the monster, allows it to live, and allows it to thrive.

Kristin and I went out regularly now. I would say that approximately 50 percent of the time she would go home before me, and I would stay out. Most of the time during this period of our relationship, I would come home two to four hours later, heavily intoxicated, but I would still work the next day. I would've never been comfortable consenting to her staying out until the late hours of the night or early hours of the next morning, knowing what I know about the bar scene. Kristin knew how I felt about adultery. Of all the bad habits I've ever had and of all the inappropriate conduct I have ever engaged in, I never smoked cigarettes or committed adultery. I find it to be repulsive. It probably has something to do with the fact that I regularly sit in my office with people who just found out that their spouse or loved one is cheating on them. For decades, I've watched the devastation of shattered dreams and the results of the violation of about the most sacred trust people can have. When people regularly come to you with their bleeding heart on their sleeve, almost unable to have a conversation because of the deep and relentless pain that they are in, I believe it's persuasive, if not downright prohibitive, that you would engage in such conduct. I've often indicated that adultery is a plague on our society, undermines one of the most sacred relationships that two people can have, and brings financial devastation to many completely innocent victims including children. Divorce and the separation of two people in a relationship equate to pain and bad math. It's bad math because two people in one household with children, getting by, can rarely get by with the required two separate households, often sharing children. Children then become empowered with the ability to persuade their parents to act in a manner on the path of least resistance because with that child support check, there's a lot of power. Kristin knew that because of my feelings and experience as a lawyer and my experience as a husband and father that cheating was never an option. But there's another type of cheating, and that's one with a bottle, which I regularly engaged in for years. Often in the house of God and the eyes and ears of our family and friends, we get married and make very serious promises. Often, those promises become secondary to alcoholism and addiction. There is no honor and cherish from a barstool—intoxicated or high—just dishonor and disrespect. I was once told that love is a verb, not a noun. I get it now, and thank God I have been given another chance to implement it.

I would typically frequent only three bars. I was well-known there, was treated very well, and if I ran out of money, they trusted me to pay at a later date. I never had to worry about anything but last call. Often, this is a sign of a sure alcoholic. I would take a bottle of vodka to go with the last call in case I needed a little more before I tried to go to sleep. The concept is a level of insanity that only an alcoholic or addict can understand. At this period of my life, if I was up, I wanted to be higher, and if I was down, I wanted to be lower. No matter where I was relative to my level of intoxication, no matter what high I had going on, I wanted more. It was never enough until the blackout. I was out of control when I was drinking and now started to live with regret and shame when I wasn't. Regret and shame are simply fuel for the next drunk. How could I not know that I was an alcoholic with this type of conduct? I would go a week or so in between binges, but once booze touched my lips, all morality and all rules that I had while sober disappeared. Kristin used to kid around and say that vodka gives me amnesia. When I drank, I would forget my address, forget that I had loved ones and children waiting for me at home, that I had to work the next day, or that I had responsibilities. That is what booze has to offer. I wish it was amnesia, but I now know I personally chose not to go home and that the grips of the disease made my decisions, guided my conduct—or should I say, misconduct.

I still tried or fought the urge to drink alone or at home. We would occasionally drink for social gatherings, and I found that to be acceptable. As misguided as my rules were, I tried very hard to live by them—an obvious attempt to prevent myself from accepting that I was abusing alcohol and drugs and the unaffordable thought process that I was an alcoholic. Unaffordable to the monster because it may jeopardize its feeding. The monster gets very protective at times such as this. During this period of time, I would often drink two bottles of vodka in one evening at a bar. It got to the point where the bartenders at my regular places would open a new bottle when I walked in. They had all witnessed my progression. There were jokes about how much I and my drinking buddies drank but no serious discussions about stopping. Once in a while after a particularly glorious showing, we would talk about taking it easy for a while. Discussions of any self-restraint usually disappeared when the hangover or headache disappeared.

Like many alcoholics, I had started with beer, then some liquor, mixing drugs in between. This progression from beer to liquor took decades. About the time of my separation, I had started with vodka cranberry club soda. Then it was vodka, one half of the glass, and one quarter cranberry and one quarter club soda. Soon it was vodka splash of cranberry. Probably to trick other people into thinking I was having a mixed drink. And at this point of my life while sitting in a bar without Kristin, straight vodka, couple ice cubes, and keep them coming until I say no more, which I never remember saying now that I think about it. This last progression only took a few years. I would tell bartenders that I shouldn't have to ask for another drink and that their tip would often reflect how many times I have to ask or not ask for a drink—a ridiculous, pompous, arrogant, and narcissistic request. Sober, I would knock my children off the chair for acting like this. Intoxicated or on my way to intoxicated, I regularly acted like this. The hypocrisy was blatant, but I couldn't see it.

Drugs were secondary at this point, and alcohol was my primary focus. Don't get me wrong; when drinking, there was plenty of drugs for all. But booze could provide for me just about everything I wanted. There was a lot of misbehavior going on each side of my barstool and mine, but of course, because I was drinking instead of voicing my opinion or objecting, I would high-five people for their inappropriate behavior. Sober, I would get up and leave the place if I thought someone was possibly going to cheat on their wife. Sober, I would get up and leave if anyone had drugs in their pocket. Intoxicated, I never met an idea that I thought was inappropriate. Add alcohol—instant immoral asshole who was morally bankrupt. Living these two separate lives started to create conflict within me. I use this conflict to drink harder and more often. Simple solution to a troubled conscience—drink. I didn't have a conscience when I was drunk, so drink and no problem? Monday-morning quarterbacking—holy shit, what an idiot. I regularly told people my IQ was above room temperature, but this conduct was contrary to that assertion by a mile. The insanity of the conduct was blatant, but again, I did not see it.

The chains of alcohol
are too light to be felt,

Until they are too strong
to be broken.

—common AA quote

CHAPTER NINE

This type of heavy drinking with regular blackouts continued for the next few years. I started to struggle with the concept that I may be abusing alcohol, so I came up with the idea that I would go longer in between binges. I had every good intention of going a week or two or thirty days without any drink. My reward to myself was another binge. Illogical, yes, but that is logical to an alcoholic or addict. Every time before the first drink during this period of time, I would promise myself, I would promise Kristin, "This time, I will only have a few, and I will go home." Kristin's patience with my drinking was very thin by this point, but I was regularly going weeks without a drink. I can't have a drinking problem if I can go two or three weeks between drinks, right? Even some of my drinking buddies at this point were starting to comment on how much I would drink when I drank. I was downing vodka like water, and the blackouts started to occur sooner during my binges. I was losing a day or two a month to blackouts. There were even a few two-day binges where I have only five minutes of memory. Two days out of the house and no calls home—hideous conduct. I still hung on to the idea that I abused alcohol, and the concept that I was an alcoholic did not even begin to seriously enter my mind. How could this be?

The more Kristin yanked at me about my drinking, the harder I would drink when I drank and the longer it would be before I would come home. It was a losing battle for her, and I was losing my battle with alcohol. The monster was laughing; it was happy and at will. The difference is that she knew she was losing me to the booze, and I had no idea that every aspect of my life was now being negatively affected by my binges. Again, I rationalize that I can't have a problem: I do not drink in the morning. I do not drink at lunch when I'm working. I do not drink alone at home. When Kristin would plead with me not to go out with the guys, the last two sounds of that argument was always the same: the door slamming behind me and the car driving off. Complete unadulterated asshole.

This is the first time, as I now recall, that alcohol seriously started to affect my conduct and actions when I was sober. I am sure the bystanders would say much sooner if they were questioned. The monster was being jeopardized as I questioned the role of alcohol in my life. It took Kristin's concern and love and twisted it, presenting itself as nagging and bitching. I would've done the same thing to a loved one who was doing what I was doing to myself. I watched my father die slowly of cancer; he was terminally ill, and there was nothing we could do about it. We watched him die with dignity. There is no dignity when the terminal illness of alcoholism is ravishing your life, your lifestyle, your loved ones, and your mind and body. I knew I was tearing myself up. I had no idea what I was doing to Kristin and my children. Alcoholism and addiction are very selfish and make you selfish. I was drinking so hard at this time that if I threw up, I joked to myself that I had more room to drink now. If insanity itself could think, it would've agreed that I was two exits past way out there.

After every single binge now, I made promises that I truly intended on keeping. I was so sincere and so broken inside. After a binge and with some type of self-awareness, I would lie in bed and pray for God to help me stop drinking. I remember questioning God: If you exist, why do you allow these substances to affect people such as myself? If you exist, why can't you help me stop drinking? If you exist and I can't stop drinking and drugging, please take me in my sleep so I can stop this cycle I am in. Letting myself down was one thing—I could always just drink to make the pain go away. Letting Kristin and my children down was another. The shame was thick now. My conscience was active with disgust for myself and guilt, and I had very little ability to parent appropriately. In between binges, I felt so bad about what I was doing that I backed off on most of the rules I had. Thank God I had wonderful kids, and they were more concerned with me and my drinking than they were with taking advantage of the situation. Kristin and my mother were pleading with me regularly to get help, and I started to consider it—when hungover.

I did not think I could live with the shame and guilt and the deceit anymore. So many nights I lay awake, going over and over in my head the events of my life that led me to the point I was at. How could I have allowed this to happen? Where was the chink in my armor? What was the inherent weakness in my personality that allowed me to take it this far? This process stripped me of the ego that allowed me to do so many positive things in my life. I was shrouded in shame and guilt and lost my self-esteem and my swagger, and I'll be damned, that made me want to drink even more.

Kristin had had enough. My children have had enough. My mother told me I was a drunk and a drug addict, and she wanted nothing to do with me unless I cleaned up. They were no longer enabling me. I was out of control. They knew it, and something horrible was bound to happen. There were no more social gatherings, just my binges. Kristin knew that we could not go out to dinner and have a few drinks. She knew how it would end. I started to withdraw significantly, and the once happy and outgoing and sometimes pompous man was now quiet, deep in his own misery, unable to laugh and smile. I knew I was struggling, but I had no idea I was in the struggle for my life. Even with all this going on, I put a few sober weeks in, and then I would feed the monster. And when a monster goes weeks without feeding, it becomes ravenous and out of control.

After one particularly bad binge, I pleaded with Kristin to get me in outpatient treatment. I didn't even sleep that night. I scared myself so bad with the last two days of drinking and drugging. The next day, I was sitting in my first meeting. I would go on and off for about six months, probably have four or five binges during that period of time. Being in treatment, as they say, and still drinking and using did nothing to help the squirrels in my head. My brain was scrambled, but I was honestly trying to clean myself up. I knew I was abusing the hell out of alcohol, and the drugs followed, but the word "alcoholic" still had not completely entered my mind.

It's impossible to believe. It's insane to imagine that with everything I've been through, that I had yet to surrender to the powerful disease that had taken all the good from my life and flushed it down the toilet. Only an alcoholic or addict could ever understand the insanity, the hypocrisy, and the downright stupidity and inconsistency of the thought process and the conduct when one is struggling with this disease.

After a few more binges, I started talking to someone in a twelve-step program about attending a meeting. I felt I was losing Kristin. I knew I'd lost her and my children's respect at this point, but they were still pulling for me. Kristin and I met with another attorney who was in the program, and we had dinner. I remember everything about that night. I was so scared. No doubt, the monster was scared, and it exhibited itself through my anxiety.

After dinner, I was taken to my first AA meeting. I listened for quite a while, and then I stood up; it was my turn to address this demon. This was my moment that I could tame the monster and put it in a cage. Everyone before me said "my name is so-and-so, and I'm an alcoholic." I proudly stood up. I was ready to confront all this, and then I spoke.

"Hello." My voice quivered. "My name is Ron, and I have a problem with alcohol."

Are you fucking kidding me? Did I really just say that? I've gone through all this to get to my first AA meeting, and I couldn't say the word "alcoholic." I clearly remember becoming dizzy and disorientated when I said that I had a drinking problem. I almost had to sit down. I was so nervous and had no idea what just happened, so I said I was just there to listen. Obviously, I hadn't surrendered yet. I hadn't hit my bottom, as they say.

I started going to meetings regularly and went for six to eight months, with four or five binges in between. Everyone knew I was trying, and that made the guilt from the binges even worse. After a particularly bad binge around thanksgiving of 2005, I swore off alcohol as I did thousands of times before, literally, and got serious about the program. My friend who brought me to my first meeting told me I needed a sponsor and that I needed to start working the steps. I was ready. I was a washcloth of a man at this point in time. I was broken. I was detached; my thoughts were scattered, and I actually thought that death was a reasonable option. I could not continue to live with this much pain, with this much shame, and with the thought that I would pick up a drink again and drink or drug. I was causing my family so much grief that anything that I had to offer positively failed in comparison to the total emotional devastation my loved ones felt. Ironically, as terrible as I felt about myself, I was still very concerned about what my loved ones thought about me. I was supposed to be the rock, the backbone of the family, the provider, and the guy with all the answers. Now I was on my knees, praying to God to help me stop drinking or to take my life in my sleep, without notice and quietly. My fall from grace was grievous and without forgiveness in my mind. I had imagined my funeral. Would my drinking buddies show up? Would they be too ashamed to look at my wife and my mother and my children? These horrendous thoughts for a man who had so many things going well in his life made me realize that I had reached bottom, that I needed to get sober, that I needed my loved ones around me, that I needed my business, that I needed myself back. I honestly felt possessed at times, thinking that there was a demon or a monster devouring all that is good inside of me. This is what it took for me to take the program seriously, and I found a sponsor and started to work the program. Desperation is a gift, and I was desperate to find answers, or else.

I remember being sober for thirty days.

I was so scared that I would go back. Working the program and hanging around with completely sober people who acted sober, I started to get my swagger back. Everyone that knew me who was part of my sober life was very supportive. My drinking buddies disappeared. No phone calls, no get-well cards, nothing. One of the first things you learn in the program is to change your playgrounds and your playmates. People, places, and things need to change to get sober. I did. I was so weak that I couldn't even watch commercial with booze or beer in it.

Then ninety days sober, what a great feeling.

I was still living with the regrets of my past and knew that I was weak and that I was not out of the woods.

Six months and then a year sober.

I remember the feeling of great accomplishment that was at my one year anniversary. I had a sober network in and out of the program; no one in the family drinks around me, and I was back on track. I actually felt that I was an even better person than I had been before. This experience had humbled me significantly. I was learning how to deal with life on life's terms—the proverbial man up and deal with life head on. They say being sober is not for sissies, and it's true. I hid behind alcohol for so long I was experiencing many new feelings and emotions. The difference was I was actually dealing with them and not hiding behind a bottle or on a barstool or drugs. My relationship with Kristin blossomed; my relationship with my children was excellent again. When they looked at me, it was obvious that they respected me and who I was, again.

Two people will hurt you:
The great "I am"
and
The "Poor me."

—common AA quote

CHAPTER TEN

I had actually put some time behind me and sobriety. I put a few twenty-four hours together, and I was looking at my second anniversary of being sober—absolutely impossible, or so I thought. Pieces of my life seemed to come back together quickly as soon as I put down the drink and the drugs. It was time to start taking care of myself, eat healthy, work out, take care of some physical issues I had. I had been limping for some time, and I had a lot of pain in my knee. I also had significant issues with my heel. Being sober helped me many ways in my life, but it did nothing for the daily pain that I lived in. The pain was excruciating at times, and occasionally, I had to walk with a cane and regularly could not participate in normal activities. No longer hiding behind alcohol and drugs, I made an appointment to see a doctor. I saw a few doctors before an expert in Albany indicated, after a number of tests, that he believed half my Achilles tendon had been torn off and that I had been walking around with one half of my Achilles tendon severed from my heel and rolled up inside of the back my calf. I was introduced to painkillers, and they helped. I took them pursuant to the prescription. I took the amount prescribed and took them consistently with the hours in between doses as prescribed. I complied with the doctor's instructions but did not consider the dangers of popping opiates regularly. Prescription opiates are just street opiates in the convenience of a prescription bottle.

I had my first surgery, and the doctor had to take a tendon out of my big toe and re-create half my Achilles, reconstructing it, drilling a hole in my heel and using the tendon from my big toe to meld together a functioning Achilles tendon. I could not do any weight-bearing for two or three months. I left the hospital with a pocket full of painkillers and a number of refills. At this point in time, I was strongly destined to be sober and was not afraid of the idle time that I would be spending with my family and actually looked forward to it. The first few weeks, I stayed home, other than a few trips to the office. I was on crutches and could not put any weight on my heel. After a few months and a few hundred painkillers or more, the cast was taken off, and I was given a walking boot. This was a painful experience, and I relied upon the painkillers. I had traded my drug of choice with a prescription although I had no idea.

My knee continued to hurt significantly. I went to a couple more doctors and was referred to a sports injury specialist. After a number of tests and being unable to diagnose the exact problem, he performed surgery on my knee but did not find any significant problems, at least not enough to support the level of pain I was having. After the surgery more painkillers not only for the surgery itself but for the significant pain and inflammation in my knee. I was limping, and obviously, the change in my gait did not help my knee. I was regularly counting on painkillers now to allow me the freedom to engage in leisure activities. I was sober, and life was reasonably good. I was dealing with life on life's terms, and I was happy. My relationships with Kristin and the kids and my family were excellent. I was working hard to do an excellent job for my clients. I felt good about myself. I was going to meetings, working with my sponsor, enjoying my sober network. I was enjoying my sober life. Life was so good that Kristin and I got married. Her one condition, my sobriety, had been accomplished. It was time to share the same last name and prepare to give her the greatest gift known to a woman . . . . Motherhood. A year after we got married Kristin was pregnant and expecting twins.

The pain continued and was becoming a constant distraction. I was actually afraid that I would get so frustrated that I would pick up a drink and get back on that train wreck to hell. When the doctor that did my first knee surgery could not help me, I was referred to another sports knee injury doctor. I was on the office table for my 2nd consult with a new doctor for three minutes or so when he twisted my leg around, and I jumped through the roof. He told me to relax and did it again. If I recall correctly, I actually clenched my fist as I wanted punch him. The first time he did it, I understood; the second time he did it, he smirked. At first, I thought he was sadistic. But I quickly realized he was proud of himself as he had discovered the source of my pain after many doctors and the surgery did not disclose. He told me my hip was bad; I laughed at him and told him I didn't have a pain in my hip but in my knee. The doctor indicated that the location of pain is not a good sign of where the injury is. That the body is full of pathways and nerves and pain can often follow them. He said, "Give me about five minutes, and we'll see." Immediately, he preformed an x-ray, and sure enough in about five minutes, he showed me the x-ray. My hip was completely shot. I'd lost significant amount of bone, and it was obvious to him that it was the source of the pain in my knee.

Enter more painkillers. We tried for a period of time to treat it with cortisone shots deep in the hip, painkillers, rest, therapy as I recall, but nothing helped. The pain was north of my knee, in the knee and started in my groin; I was limping worse than ever. The decision was made to take my hip and give me a hip implant. The doctor indicated that it was actually easier for the elderly to have hip replacements as they have far less muscle mass. As a former athlete who would work out at the gym regularly, I had a lot of thigh muscle to go through. I had the surgery, and I was filleted like a fish. The doctor indicated the average hip replacement surgery would require a six-inch scar. Mine was closer to eighteen inches, and he indicated that he had a significant amount of trouble getting the hip in because I was a large man with very thick thigh muscle. Regardless, I was in pain and required more painkillers. I was given Percocet for the first time. The doctor indicated it was much stronger, but for some reason, I preferred the Lortab (also known as hydrocodone).

I continued to have significant inflammation and pain in my knee and months after the hip replacement, even after the hip should have healed, the pain was worse than ever in my knee. The doctor tried multiple cortisone shots, but they didn't touch the pain. I continued the painkillers, but they became ineffective. The pain was keeping me up at night. I was exhausted. I was limping, and I was wearing thin. The monster was calling to me, and I was scared. It wanted to use this situation to make me pick up, but I insisted I would not. I recall the struggle in my head as the frustration of the pain continued. I'd now had three surgeries, and my pain was worse than before. The doctor sent me to a couple of his partners who came to the same conclusion that they understood that there was something going on in my knee but had no idea what. I was finally referred to another one of the doctor's partners who specialized in knees and worked regularly with athletes at a local college. The doctor felt the issue was under the kneecap and that the limping and the change in my gait for so long had ruined the cartilage under my kneecap and that the kneecap was bone on bone with the bottom of my femur. He indicated it was complicated because the top of the femur was now replaced with titanium and plastic.

I continued the painkillers and believe I was given an increased dosage. I was also getting painkillers from a general physician at this time as my surgeons were an hour away. The doctor did my second knee surgery, which was now about two years after my first surgery. While on the table and while awake, watching the surgery on a monitor, the doctor bent my leg and showed me what was happening. The doctor indicated that my leg, once bent, had no cartilage under my knee and the knee cap was bone on bone with the femur. He said this is not uncommon for unequal leg syndrome, when people have lost bone from hips. Once people's gait changes, the kneecap tracks differently. He cleaned up the bottom of the kneecap and performed surgery, hoping to give me the relief I needed. Months after the surgery, I was still in pain and taking pain medications. My pain was a little better at times but not much better. The doctors thought that by lengthening my femur when they did the hip, it may have tightened my quad muscles, which pulled the kneecap down tighter on my femur. They decided to do a third knee surgery. I had the third knee surgery, and the doctor did a lateral release and cut some of the quad muscles to allow the knee cap to free float on one side. Of course, I continued the painkillers.

By now I've been on painkillers on or off for a couple years. The lateral release relieved some of the pain but not all of it. I still wasn't sleeping nights from the pain in my hip and my knee, and the painkillers helped a lot during the day. I had no idea at this time that I was absolutely addicted to painkillers and that my body was craving it like it used to crave alcohol and other drugs. Painkillers are cocaine and heroine in a pill, provided by your doctor. This process made it less likely that I would ever consider I was an addict until disaster occurred.

I was getting painkillers from the doctors in Albany before surgery, at or about the time of surgery, and after surgery. Five surgeries scattered between about twenty-four months: painkillers before, during the twenty-four months, and after. I was also getting painkillers from my local doctor, and I honestly came to a point where I couldn't live without them. Just like alcohol, it snuck up on me, and I had no idea I was in full-blown addiction to pain killers which is like heroin in a pill. During this period of time, studies were provided to assist doctors in dealing with opiate addictions. I started doctor-shopping. That, of course, would come to an end, and I was down to one doctor providing me opiates. Our twins were born during this period of time and we were overloved and blessed by them.

There's a lot less shame with popping a pill than sitting on a barstool. I struggled with the concept that I was an opiate addict, but it was prescribed by a doctor, so how bad could it be? I had a bottle with those in it, with my name and the doctor's name on it. It wasn't alcohol or street drugs, I argued with myself. The reality was my addiction to pain pills was as bad (if not worse) by this point than it ever was with alcohol. With booze, I didn't drink every day and binged horribly when I drank at the end. With pills, I needed them daily to function. When I didn't have any, I started to feel lethargic and irritable. My pain level was actually getting worse, and I had reasoned in my mind that the arthritis just continued to ravage my leg. I later learned that this is simply the body's response to force the addict to feed the monster more opiates. The monster may have its choice of substance, but deny it one, and it will live off another.

Addiction is addiction, and after I stop feeding the monster alcohol, it had no problem taking the opiates in its place. Easy to come by in my circumstances—easy to get from a doctor, easy to get the prescription increased because the pain level continued, and (I was soon to realize) easy to get on the street when you couldn't get enough from the doctor. I started getting pills from other people who had prescriptions. I was soon buying them regularly on the street. Again, I reasoned. Doctors prescribe it every day, and they've given it to me for a few years—how bad could it be? I was taking a tremendous amount of pills every day now, and my body had built up serious tolerance to the dosage. Like a typical opiate addict, I started with four per day. That increased to six per day. Then they upped the dosage, and the new dose was four per day, and then soon, six per day. That I was doubling up six times a day.

Addiction is, of course, progressive, and it wasn't long before I was taking three or four pills every couple hours just to quell the pain and so that I could feel good. I was so physically addicted that when I didn't have pills, when I didn't have opiates in my body, I couldn't sleep enough. Probably the only time in my life that I've slept long periods of time was when I didn't have pills, and I was in withdrawal from the opiates. This, of course, is not refreshing sleep, and you don't wake up feeling well. You wake up sicker than hell, looking for the next dose.

I was slamming these pills like Skittles. There were days that I would take dozens and dozens. I was withdrawing, and I believe that the pain was worse; the pleasure center of my brain was shutting down. I was depressed and had almost no ability to enjoy life unless I was chewing on a couple of opiate pills and swallowing them down. The chase to get the pills became a daily chore and was time-consuming and financially devastating. My opiate habit was costing me $1,000 a week or more. I didn't even care about paying my bills or taking care of myself or my family. I was in full-blown addiction, feeding the monster, just doing it differently this time.

With the self-realization that I was an addict, the shame started to keep me away from AA meetings. Ironic, when I needed my sober network the most, I excluded them in my daily routine and withdrew because I was sure that they would figure out what was going on. Everybody knew I had all the surgeries; everyone had seen the scars, the crutches, the cast, etc. But the surgeries were done. No one could have ever understood how or why I was taking so many pills. I was once again living as a hypocrite, and the shame and guilt was back.

Of course, this is just more fuel for the monster, and the conflict within me made me crave more opiates. The exact same cycle—different substance but the same emotions leading to financial, personal, physical, emotional, and spiritual devastation and ruin. How could I allow this to happen to me again? The first time, I didn't see it. The first time, I didn't know addiction was a progressive disease. The first time, I was completely unaware that there was free help and sober networks out there with people willing to lay down their lives to help you. With all that knowledge and with so many people in the program and in my life who would help me—how could I get to this point again? I was beyond distraught. I was less than the shell of a man, and I believe I was far lower than I was when I put down the bottle.

Kristin was all over me to put down the pills. My mother, brother, and children knew that something was wrong with me, and they were regularly questioning me on whether I was drinking or taking drugs. I even talked to my doctor a few times about weaning off the pills, but I was not strong enough to do it on my own. I knew I needed help, but my disease and addiction to opiates—identical to addiction to alcohol—lied to me, coaxed me to take more pills. Addiction is cunning and baffling, and I was baffled. The more distraught I got, the more I needed the pills, or so I justified. The more distraught I got, the worse the pain, the more I needed the pills—a familiar cycle in my life. This time, I actually wondered if it was possible to beat it. I beat it once when I had no idea what I was facing at first. If it snuck up on me again in a different form (this time in opiates), how could I beat it? I tried really hard for six months, and every single time I put down the pills or tried to wean down, I got so sick that I could not function. Kristin pleaded with me to check myself into a rehab or a detox center or hospital. I, of course, declined because I was confident that willpower alone could get me through. Same denial I had with alcohol. Same result.

It was so easy getting sober the first time I must not understood or appreciated that. With complacency comes relapse. I had lost the gift of desperation. Relapse comes in many forms, and it can sneak up on you in many ways. Mine was as predictable as the sun coming up tomorrow, but I had no idea. A strong weapon of the monster is denial and complacency, and they act as a type of misdirection. Take your attention from the hard work to get and stay sober, and the monster feeds again.

My second trip to hell was just as bad, if not worse than the first. This time, I had far less excuses because I've been sober, I've sought treatment, and I've surrounded myself with people who were sober and would help me stay sober. I now knew what I needed to do; I had all the resources but did not avail myself of them. This is inexcusable. I had none of the tragic emotional triggers of the first time. Some alcoholics and addicts like me hit bottom, then grab a shovel, and dig deeper yet. And that is what I did, and I dug and dug and dug.

The only weapon
that becomes sharper with
constant use
is the tongue.

—common AA quote

CHAPTER ELEVEN

I felt down and out again and out of control. My attempts to stop taking the pills were failures. I was right back where I started. But now I had alienated my sober network; I had stopped going to meetings. I was a huge hypocrite, and this time, I was dancing a familiar step and went into it with all the knowledge of the disease of addiction. I had no excuse. I reasoned that no one in AA would help me. After all, I had stopped going to meetings and was a hypocrite. The program and the people who helped me so much to put down the bottle, I had convinced myself, would not give me a second chance. The reality is that it is a program of many chances and full of very patient, caring, and courageous people who are always there. But I had let them down. I let my family down. I let myself down. These are thoughts of a man who is led around by a beast deep within himself, whispering nonsense in his ear. I swear it is like being schizophrenic. I couldn't even look in the mirror. I was again talking to God nights when I couldn't sleep and would pray on occasion. I couldn't take the pain and guilt anymore. My marriage was in trouble. My business was suffering, and everyone that knew me knew something serious was happening. But I, of course, was unable or unwilling to ask for help. Addiction makes you do the most illogical things that you can imagine. I think it's a disease of opposites. If a sober person would go left under certain circumstances, an alcoholic or addict would go right and so on. The turmoil and bad decisions create the triggers that help to maintain the insanity. That's just the way it is: anything to feed the monster, anything to keep you off-kilter so that you cannot gather yourself and get help and beat the disease. This relapse was unforgivable to me, and I was failing and falling fast.

I thought that I would make one last attempt to go off the pills on my own. I was somewhere between a half a day to a day without pills, and I was violently ill. Kristin pleaded with me to check myself in some place, but I was going to do this at home on my own and without anyone knowing. In hindsight, this is a medical issue; an opiate addiction is not handled at home. I had a great idea, or so I thought at the time. What if I just drank for a few days until I get these pills out of my system? Would my old friend alcohol help me through this? Just enough to get me by—that is what I thought.

My law partner had just left and had taken my paralegal; my wife is threatening to take the twins, so what else can I do? I did the next logical thing for an alcoholic addict who's a complete asshole: I bought a bottle of vodka. I remember clearly the dreadful moment I put that glass to my lips. The monster promised me from whispers within my head that this was the answer. The shame and guilt picking up dissipated immediately when that vodka went down my throat into my body. It was straight vodka. I was not going to dilute it with mixes; it was cheap vodka, but to me, it was smooth and welcomed. I do not remember why I bought cheap vodka. I immediately—literally—started to feel better. And so I drank and I drank. My wife took the twins and went to her mother's so she didn't have to witness my self-destruction or death. I was so angry that my law partner, paralegal, and wife had turned their backs on me that I was prepared to drink myself to death and say fuck them all. I justified that I had solely been responsible for their jobs, and they left the firm. I was the sole bread earner at our home, and my wife went to her mother's. No intervention? They never sat down like they do on TV when everyone that cares about you holds hands and cries and tells you about how much they love you. No, instead they bailed on me. I had taken care of all these people for so many years, and I was now alone in life. Again, the ranting, illogical thoughts of a man harboring a demon host. The monster laughed. "Drink from the bottle and piss on their graves someday." That is what it said. My self-pity party and resentment brought me to a moment where I picked up a bottle of booze after years of being sober, but a few of those years, I was popping pills like candy.

I reasoned that I had been through so much prior to picking up that bottle of vodka. No more and no less than the average person goes through. I look back, and it probably was the most necessary thing for me to take this disease seriously and get to a point where I was at bottom again. And oh, don't forget to dig deeper once you hit bottom. This time, I had a bigger shovel, and I was digging feverishly. I was mad, and by the rejection of my wife, my law partner, and my paralegal, I had enough resentment to fuel the binge for a long while. Even my son who was still living with me went to stay at his mother's, and he was twenty years old. I had the house to myself. Self-pity, resentment, and vodka—that was all I needed. Enter, my old drinking buddies.

I picked up the phone and, lo and behold, got a hold of an old drinking buddy who was more than happy to come sit and talk with me. He was also more than happy to drink and drug with me. I don't blame him; I made these choices, and I made the choice to get as messed up as I could. I wasn't going to go to a bar this time, was not in the mood to let strangers witness my self-destruction. I won't go as far saying I was suicidal, but I was prepared to drink myself into oblivion. I would deal with the damage later. I was at risk of losing everything that mattered to me: my wife and my children. And my business was in serious jeopardy. Instead of facing these problems head-on and getting help, I chose to pick up a vodka bottle. This would be the biggest of all binges. This would be historic. They would write folk songs about this one, my monster told me. I did not let my monster's expectations down.

I've been feeding the monster opiates for a while, but now its best friend alcohol was back. It was savage and ravenous, and I couldn't get enough. I went to a couple of different liquor stores and purchased booze over the next few days. I didn't want to go to one liquor store and buy all that alcohol in one spot. I was trying not to call too much attention to myself. After I got really tanked, I went over to my buddy's house in fear that someone would come to my house and there would be a confrontation. I was on a mission, and nothing was going to stand in my way. It amazes me that I don't remember ever once thinking about pulling back. I was a couple bottles of vodka deep the first night. I was drinking and drugging like the old days, and I'll be honest, I was so messed up that any guilt and shame was far behind me, Resentment fueled me, and for a little while, it felt good. I got a few hours of sleep and started my next day around 6:00 am with vodka and gin for breakfast. I wasn't taking pills, I reasoned. I think I drank myself into a partial coma by 9:00 am and had to take a nap. I went home and was sleeping when my wife had sent some of our police friends over to check on me. They tried to reason with me that what I was doing was wrong, that I was letting my family down, my wife and children, that I wasn't doing anything healthy for my business or myself. I told them I appreciated their input and concern but I had the constitutional right to act like an asshole. After they left, I knew I shouldn't stay home much longer, so I took off and got more booze and went and hung out with my drinking buddy. I drank the entire day and drugged the entire day until the early morning hours the next day when I slept again for a few hours. If it's possible, I may have outdone myself on this binge. My body was rejecting the fact that it did not have opiates, but the more I drank, the less that rejection was felt by me. I had stopped sweating and shivering after the first two bottles of vodka. The diarrhea soon stopped too. I wasn't puking anymore, and I was keeping all the booze down. Withdrawals from opiates is ugly. I kept telling myself I would just drink until I get through this opiate withdraw. All this could have been avoided in a hospital or a rehab or a detox center, but I was not taking cues from reason, logic, or common sense. I was taking them from the monster.

I was in this cycle for three-and-a-half days when my wife took drastic actions to get me help. She and my brother, with the help and assistance of some of my actual friends, called the police and reported that I was passed out on the couch in my house and reported that I threatened to harm myself. They were told this was the only way that they could bring me to a hospital and get me help. Apparently, they indicated I threatened to kill myself. My conduct may have been consistent with that, but those words never came out of my mouth. It was a Friday afternoon, and I had been out since early Tuesday morning on my binge. I awoke to about six police officers standing over me, EMTs, and volunteer firemen. Apparently, the caller over the scanner unresponsive male at my address, possible threat of suicide. This of course, in a small town in scanner land, would lead to ridiculous rumors of my demise and untimely death.

Waking up from a blackout on your couch—still intoxicated—to many police in your living room is an experience I would not wish on anyone. They tried to reason with me that they were going to take me to the hospital. The conversation did not go well, and at one point, an officer grabbed my arm, and I told him that I was ready to take them all on and that this would not end well, all of us would be on the floor and ugly. I told him that the report was false and that I had not done anything to justify their intrusion into my home. Luckily for me, one of my very good friends was a police officer and came to the call, in essence to protect me. He pleaded with me to go quietly that they would not handcuff me, and he would personally take me to the hospital. He indicated that at this point, even if the report was untrue, they had no choice and that three-and-a-half days of being drunk was enough. I agreed to walk out with him and him alone. I got outside, and all the neighbors were there. It seemed like a hundred cars with flashing lights were there—a ridiculous scene in my small neighborhood. I saw my wife and my brother standing together, and I told them that they were dead to me and that I never wanted anything to do with them again. If there wasn't a dozen or so cops around, I probably would've taken a hand to my brother. At that moment, I never hated any person more as I was told he was the one who made the phone call. In reality, it was my wife and my brother plotting to attempt to save me. I could not fathom why my wife was not by my side. The reality was she was taking the drastic step to pull me back from hell on Earth.

I spent about eight hours in the hospital, being interviewed. My mother, my wife, and brother were there. I would only talk to my mother at this time as I was seething with anger that my wife and my brother called the police. My blood-alcohol level was so high that I had to wait hours before they deemed me to be competent to have an intelligent conversation. I lay there ashamed and became angrier and angrier with every person that walked by my room that knew me. The two police officers outside my room made it very clear that I wasn't there for your typical in and out hospital visit. I was eventually released, and I was brought home by my wife and brother about midnight. I asked my wife if she was going to stay at the house with me, but she declined unless I agreed to go to detox or rehab. I told her I didn't need to go, that I've been days without pills, and that I was over it. She dropped me off to an empty house. That night, embarrassed, hurt, and lonely, my resentment grew again. It was different this time; the public embarrassment would not let me sleep.

I arose early the next morning. I guess I had not had enough because I found a way to grab another couple of bottles, even without transportation and before the liquor stores open. Alcoholics and addicts are very resourceful. I was a bottle of vodka and a few beers deep before I decided to call my wife. I told her I'd had enough, that I cannot go on like this, and that I would go to rehab or detox that day. I just need a little time to collect myself. I don't think she knew I was intoxicated again at that moment. It was only about 10:00 am. I had moments of lucidity through the resentment and shame, and I could not believe that after the four days I just had that I would pick up a bottle again and drink my breakfast hours after being released from the hospital. This goes far beyond any insanity I ever experienced before. I was alone. I was broken in many different ways, and it was time to surrender to my disease once again.

As I watched the darkness descend, the distinction between sky and land disappeared. The murky gray color covered the landscape as if a blanket were smothering my existence. It suddenly grew very cold, and although seemingly impossible, I felt more alone than my life ever allowed before. The darkness entered the room, and the depths of my emptiness felt its presence. It brought me back, back so far that I curled up in a corner much like the position I occupied in my mother's womb so many years ago. While familiar questions raced through my frustrated mind that night, I again realized my quest for an answer may never be over. I prayed over and over for God to take me quietly, without pain. I have suffered enough. My prayers went unanswered again.

With the beginning of each day, we ask the same questions. We pray for answers; we beg to be shown the way to a better life. Alone and broken each night we ask, we pray for a way out, a way to stop the cycle of destruction, loneliness and shame. Thousands of times I have repeated this conduct, but for so long now, my futile struggle moved me further away from that which I strongly craved to obtain. Each day my conduct, although aware of it being ill-advised, brought me to a dark and pathetic place. I cannot escape myself. I cannot forgive myself. Hopeless, hollow and beat-up, I surrender once again in defeat. And so the cycle continues.

Two hours later, I was picked up by a mutual friend who was a counselor and who my wife had confided in. I actually trusted her and knew that her qualifications as my friend and a counselor gave her a little more insight about what I was going through. She picked me up, with my mother following, and drove me an hour to a detox center. After we got there, she stayed with me for hours while they checked me in. I was scared; my shame and embarrassment had stripped me of any backbone. I was mush. That day and the next two days would be very educational and would shock my understanding, the path I was on again.

**We are sick people
trying to get better,**

**Not bad people
trying to be good.**

—common AA quote

CHAPTER TWELVE

My time in detox was my Charles Dickens's *A Christmas Carol* experience. I may not have been visited by three ghosts, but I'd absolutely seen my future, and the words "dismal future" would not be an extraordinary exaggeration. I learned more about my disease and addiction from the misery of others and their stories in that detox center than anyone could imagine. I've heard the stories so many times in the twelve-step program; maybe I wasn't listening. If I was listening, I didn't hear what was being said. I was in the program, waiting to hear the message that would bring me to the promise land, but it was not the details on the path to sobriety that I should've been listening to. It was in the details of the path to self-destruction that I should've been listening to. The experience of others was the message, the lesson—sobriety, the results; continued sobriety, the quest. How could I've missed all this?

I spent most of my first day at detox just checking in and getting settled. I was sweating and sleeping and detoxing probably still from pills and, now definitely, from the alcohol. I felt like I had a terrible flu; all I wanted to do was sleep. Groggy and feeling like crap slightly before midnight, they brought in another individual and put him in the bed next to me. That night, he sweated, cried, screamed out, shook, had seizures, flopped around like a fish, and puked. Withdrawals are a horrible thing to witness. But I was in no mood to be sympathetic as I was dealing with my own demons. I remember the nurses coming in the middle of night to check on him and had a discussion about hospitalizing him because his withdrawal symptoms were so bad. I actually became afraid to fall asleep as I had no idea what the stranger was capable of doing in his current state. I had no idea that he was blind and was as scared as I. I came to learn that he was going through horrible withdrawal symptoms from alcohol alone, and watching and hearing him going through withdrawals was painful and a window to reality. Neither my monster nor my disease could minimize what I was seeing.

I could hear people up and down the hall all night long. I was afraid to meet anyone. I was in a very antisocial mood. I just spent the last four-and-a-half days coming off opiates. I was sick and sweaty and hadn't showered. I had drunk copious amounts of alcohol that past five days. I was in no mood to make new friends. During the night, I was given methadone to help the opiate withdrawals. I was scared to death of taking it as I've heard how many people are addicted to methadone. I took the first dose because the nurses said that my blood pressure and heart rate were showing signs of withdrawals. I took the second dose for the same reason. I refused all other doses thereafter. They gave me some type of patch to help mellow me, and I was satisfied with that. Every few hours, the nurses would yell out "medicine" or something like that, and many in detox would line up to get their methadone fix. All night long, I would hear people asking the nurses when the next medicine was going to be given and that they were in a bad way and needed theirs sooner. People were groveling and complaining to take methadone while they were in detox to get off other drugs. I knew this seemed odd but wasn't really mentally capable to grasp the concept until much later. They lined up like animals at a feeding troth to get more poison.

The next morning, I was starving and went to have breakfast. My roommate, looking like hell and probably feeling worse, came into the breakfast room, bumped into something, and sat down next to me. He said, "Friend,"—he did not know I was his roommate—"could you tell me what's on my breakfast tray? I'm blind, and I need to know what food is on my plate and tray." That was the first I realized that I was sitting next to an individual with far more right to be angry at the world than I had. I wondered if he used his blindness as an excuse or if that's what caused his resentment so that he could feed his monster. I told him what was on his plate, where it was located, and he ate. We spoke and he told me his drug of choice was alcohol and alcohol alone and that he had been in and out of detox and rehab centers many times. He was tired of the cycle and wanted to stop. I guess he found his bottom again. How many times can someone hit bottom? Can it truly be the bottom if you go there numerous times?

I, of course, started to talk to the other individuals at the breakfast table and immediately struck up a conversation with two people who seemed to be just like me. Both had actually owned their own construction businesses. They were well spoken. They were kind, and they were hurting just like I was. Throughout that day, I spent many hours talking with these two guys. They both drank and drugged for years, and their stories were almost identical to mine. The difference was that they were a year or two, in my opinion, past my current situation on the road to self-destruction. Both of these guys told me a story of how their alcohol and pill addiction led them to street drugs, but alcohol and opiate pills were their drug of choice. I thought rehab and detox was for crack addicts, heroin addicts and coke addicts. Seven of the eight people I sat with that morning had the same pill and alcohol addiction I had. All of us had used many drugs, but my disease and addiction were almost identical to my new detox mates.

My two new friends told me a story of how they were successful and had houses, expensive vehicles, boats, and Jet Skis and were living the good life. Both told me how the pills and booze brought them to a place where they no longer cared to show up at the work site or take care of their respective businesses and that their sole focus was getting high and drunk. Each had lost their business, had little to do with their family members and children, and surrounded themselves with people who drank and drugged just like they did. I had lived the story and identified well. Each of them had lost their business and found financial devastation a year or two prior to being in detox with me. They were just like me; I was just like them, and I would end up just like them if I didn't get it right this time. They say misery loves company, but their misery was one of my biggest lessons. How sad. At this point in time, I was so humiliated and basically ready to do almost anything to get sober and get my life back. Maybe that's why their stories meant so much to me. I had heard similar stories in the program, but apparently, I was not ready to grasp and appreciate the lesson. I know that society would look at these guys and look at them as has-beens or throwaways, but they were wonderful people who loved and cared for others like I do—or like I did—and that their addiction had led them down a path of financial and emotional destruction that would shake a devout Christian's belief in God. They were living on other people's couches without any money, doing anything they could to feed their monster. One of the guys had been in detox ten or so times in the last ten years. This scared the hell out of me as I did not, nor could I, allow this to be a revolving door. I needed to do this one time and one time only, and I needed to get it right. I was scared to death and listening intently to the stories of where I was headed from people who were already there. It was like being able to look at my own future and see where I was going. I now know that the misery of their story was a gift to me. How sad that their misery and loss was my gateway to take my addiction serious.

One of the ladies in detox told me her story of how she started with booze, coke, and then crack. But she preferred booze and pills over all of it. There was a common theme for the people in detox here with me: we all tried just about everything, and we'd all settled on booze and pills. Was this an epidemic in our society? Why the combination? Addiction was addiction, and these two substances seemed to go hand in hand.

Another man I met was a professional pool player from Florida. He had relatives in New York, so he came to detox in New York. I asked him why he would come from Florida and travel to New York for detox, and he told me that Florida had pill mills where you would pay the doctor for a doctor's visit and be guaranteed a script of 360 pills: Lortab, Oxycodone, or OxyContin. He told me how he took the time-release OxyContins and ground them up and took the blue particles of the pill out and then heated up the powder like heroine and shot it.

I was mortified. A few years before this moment, this man's playing pool and making a living out of it and having fun, and now he's in detox for shooting or taking OxyContin and washing it down with booze. I was speechless. He started by simply taking his prescription just like me. Another story of where I was going. No one seemed to be lying; no one was bragging. These were people just like me who had lost more than I had lost, and through their honesty and their misery and their pain, I was learning from their stories. Their stories and consequences became my lesson. I had so many emotions running through me that I was almost numb. I was numb from what I was learning, and I was scared to death about the damage I've done to my family and my business. I was having anxiety about the last few years, and I was scared beyond belief about where I was headed and what would happen if I ever picked up a bottle or pills again or any other substance.

Some of the people in detox were still sweating, having diarrhea; there were in need of medical attention. Others were just comfortable being there, a place where they can't use, taking their methadone to get through the cravings and to beat the grip that their drug of choice had them in. I was mortified by my past conduct. I was horrified by what I had done to myself and my family. I was physically exhausted from the binge and coming off the opiates. I was sick in so many layers I questioned whether I could go on. But meeting these people was a revelation; not only did I discover where I would be if I didn't stop, I came to the revelation that maybe finally, I was no different than anyone else in that detox center or the program and that my IQ, my tax bracket, my station in life had nothing to do with beating or cheating my disease and taming the monster. As an alcoholic addict, I'd often thought that I was different than others and that I would treat it differently and cure myself differently. Possibly for the first time in my life, although struggling with these addictions for years, I realized I was very humbled by the knowledge that every single person, regardless of their station in life, suffers from the disease the same. We all end up a similar place—the grave or homeless—regardless of what career or job we had before the full grip of our addiction takes place.

My third day in detox was spent talking to the doctors about the physical addiction of opiates, psychological addition of alcohol, and obviously mixing the two. My blood pressure and heart rate were adequate for release, and I had newfound energy and intense anxiety. I needed to get back to my office and my family to try to patch things up. I had all the good intentions in the world, and I'd learn so much in detox. I was ashamed of where I was in life that I was so afraid of where I was headed. But I was determined to do the next right thing.

I was released from detox and had my wife and oldest daughter meet me and bring me home. My wife had promised me that if I went to detox, she would be home for me and that she and my children would be there when I get home and would stay with me and work with me. This was the promise that cemented my agreement to go to detox. Unfortunately when I got home, she dropped me off and went back to her mother's. No homecoming? No wife, no children, just an empty home and a very damaged alcoholic addict who had a lot of healing to do and a lot of damage to undo. I felt betrayed by my wife, and the monster started talking to me. I was blind to what I had put her through, her fears, her concerns as a wife and mother. I could not see beyond my own dilemma. I was at risk again, and I was alone—a recipe for relapse.

Religion is for people who are afraid they will go to hell.

Spirituality is for people who have been there.

—common AA quote

CHAPTER THIRTEEN

The first night at home, my mother and some family members came home and had a barbeque for me. My wife and two youngest children, the twins, were not there. I placed a smile on my face although the monster and I wanted to drink or drug or both. I think I was more wounded than I was on the road to detox when I felt that almost seven billion people were watching me and calling me a failure, mocking me and laughing at me ("There goes the lawyer who's a drug addict alcoholic"), I felt more betrayed than I could even imagine.

I . . . I . . . I . . . I . . . I. "I" is all I could think about. The selfishness and reasons of the disease, utilized to make me drink and drug. I couldn't get beyond it. I felt it to be the greatest betrayal. When everyone left that night, my oldest daughter stayed, and if not, I would have absolutely got a bottle or two. I would have punished my wife for not being there. I would have punished her and the twins even though they were only two. They weren't there for me when I needed them. Of course, how quickly I forgot how I hadn't been there for almost two years for them. I was a shell of a man, chasing my addiction, running from it, hiding from it, and feeding it to the detriment of my family and myself.

Regardless of the lack of reason and common sense my current emotional state had, I was at as much risk of picking up a drink as I was before leaving for detox.

I slept very little that night. I was so angry and so full of resentment that I dreamed about drinking just to piss my wife off. When I did awake in the morning, I went in very early to the office in an attempt to start to unravel the damage that I had done and rebuild my business in hopes of the new energy of trying to be sober and clean, without office staff, and to come up with a new plan. I spent the entire day going through the entire office and reevaluating every single aspect of it: from the computer systems to the computer programs to staffing issues, the type of work that I wanted to do, to be less paperwork-orientated and to be more profitable per hour. I actually had energy about me that day that was very positive, and I was very focused. I felt great shame and hid in my office and decided not to start reaching out to people by phone, be it for business or personal reasons.

As soon as I got home that evening though, my energy eluded me; my house was empty, and I was alone—the type of despair that allows an alcoholic to pick up a drink easily.

About 5:30, I didn't know if I could honestly get through the evening with the emotions that I had racing through my brain and my heart. I went to the liquor store, and I got a bottle and put it in my car. Just then, I discovered that my daughter and my two oldest sons were going to come over and have dinner with me that evening and hang out and spend some time with me. The concept of getting drunk and letting them down forced me to drive to the back of my office and dump the entire bottle without taking a sip. I don't know if it was fate or God's little shove of sunshine in my direction, but the call that my three oldest kids would be spending the evening with me, them knowing that my wife and the twins were not home with me after detox, gave me incredible hope and made me realize that my self-pity party was very misplaced. I actually had a wonderful evening with my older children. The next few days were the same: working extraordinarily hard at the firm, working from home in the evenings, and spending quality time with my older children. That week, the more time I spent with my older children and the more we laughed and talked about the issues at hand, the more I pulled back from my wife. I actually came to a point after a few days where I didn't think I wanted her home. That would be a wonderful punishment for her betrayal. Alcoholism and the emotions that surround it and the voice of the monster is very selfish and relentless in not realizing the pain and damage that others suffer at the hands of the disease. A few times that week, when I felt alone or angry or resentful, I thought about drinking. When I was busy working, when I was with my older children and laughing and enjoying their company, I didn't want to drink. It was these damn emotions that I realized were triggers. After all these years, I never understood that these simple emotions that we all have in life act as trigger points for alcoholics and addicts. The simplest, most basic emotions that are common and maybe even necessary for our own survival are used by the monster to feed itself.

I again started going to meetings that week, and a few sober friends came out of the woodwork and realized that things would be okay as long as I could stay away from the drink. That week, the twins turned two, and I went to my in-laws for their two-year-old birthday party. I was obviously very upset that it wasn't at the home that my wife and I had raised them in, but I had actually started to understand her dilemma. As an alcoholic, I could always look at the disease and blame the disease for my conduct—or misconduct as the case may be. The collateral damage of the disease is much harder to understand. I had failed to give my wife any credit for her attempt to protect herself and our twins and potentially our marriage, to ensure that I was serious about sobriety and about being clean. I was so self-absorbed with dealing with my pain and misery and selfishly averted this.

After a week and a half, my wife started asking if she could come home. At that point, I don't know if its pride or just pure vindictiveness, but I told her that the choice may no longer be hers and that she can't simply leave me after detox in violation of her promise and then just come home a week and a half later because I was working hard at the firm. In my heart, I wanted her home with the kids. After a few days of this dangerous emotional game, my wife came home. The kids were ecstatic to be home; my older kids were ecstatic to have them home. I was unsure of the destiny of the future of my wife and me. All the thought, all the anger, all the resentment and lying awake at night for that two weeks melted away immediately a few hours after she was home, and she put her arms around me and put her head on my shoulder. It was like a switch had gone off, and I was like a blubbering idiot, madly in love with this woman that days before I was willing to give a send-off and remain sober and clean without her to prove to her that she had made the wrong decision—how ridiculously infantile. With only a few weeks under my belt sober and clean and still dealing with the significant damage of my life and my business, my partner in life was now back at my side, working at the firm days with me, taking care of the home and the kids, working with me nights from home when needed. She was as cautiously optimistic as I was because I had made a promise to be sober and clean a thousand times before; honestly, I don't think I had another run in me. I don't know if I could survive another binge. I don't think my marriage could survive another go at the booze, and I don't think that my relationship with my children and the respect that they had for me for trying so hard to be clean and sober would outweigh the shame that they would have for me if I picked up again.

Wounded, hurt, and embarrassed, I was now surrounded by my family and many good friends, and together, we worked on my sobriety. They say it takes a village to raise a child. But it definitely takes a village to get someone sober and help keep them sober. I shudder to think that there are so many brothers and sisters of mine suffering from addiction that don't have the support network that I had. Getting sober and clean was one of the hardest things I have ever done, but I did it by the grace of God and the dedication of so many wonderful people. How could anyone without a home, a business, a wife and beautiful children, a mother, family members and friends and sober network get sober? I was struggling, scared to relapse with everything in the world pointing in the right direction and everything to live for and stay sober for.

I have completely surrendered to my disease and know that, at any moment, it could sneak up on me and take my life or everything that has value for me.

Yesterday I struggled and I suffered, today,
although marred by my experience, I am beautiful.

CHAPTER FOURTEEN

I am coming up on two years sober and clean. I have matured and educated myself and learned that I have many triggers that get the monster talking. I actually say to myself often, "No thanks. I tried it your way, and I was a drink, pill, or drug away from losing everything that ever mattered to me."

It may seem crazy, but addiction is insanity.

I have been blessed and continue to be blessed with sober family and friends who are vested in my sobriety. They care even though I have seriously tested their love and patience. I do not take it for granted and firmly believe I have no more chances to ever relapse and end up being so fortunate again.

Relapse means death to me, or worse. I need to always remember that. I need to fast-forward the romanticized thoughts of a drink or drug and skip directly to the dire consequences to fully comprehend the unfathomable thought of that drink or drug. I need to combat the monster daily with a prayer each morning to ask to be sober and clean for the day and be thankful at night for helping me do it. One day at a time, I stay sober, act sober, and try to lead by example.

I have many chinks in my armor, fewer now thanks to counseling groups and a twelve-step program and those in the rooms of AA. I have tremendous gratitude that there resources have saved my life, gave me my family back, gave me myself back.

I have the recipe for a sober life; now I need to remember every day the misery that awaits with one drink, one pill, one drug. I need to remember every day the principles that my sober network, friends, and family insist: I have a disease that is in remission. It takes work and prayer every day to keep it in remission. I now have no excuse. I am accountable.

I was once given the gift of desperation. I was guided by others who walked the road to hell before me. They reached into the flames of my self-destruction and pulled me out. Total strangers, friends, and family all uniting to get one middle-aged alcoholic/addict to put down the drink—no doubt a miracle.

16845664R00054

Made in the USA
Middletown, DE
22 December 2014